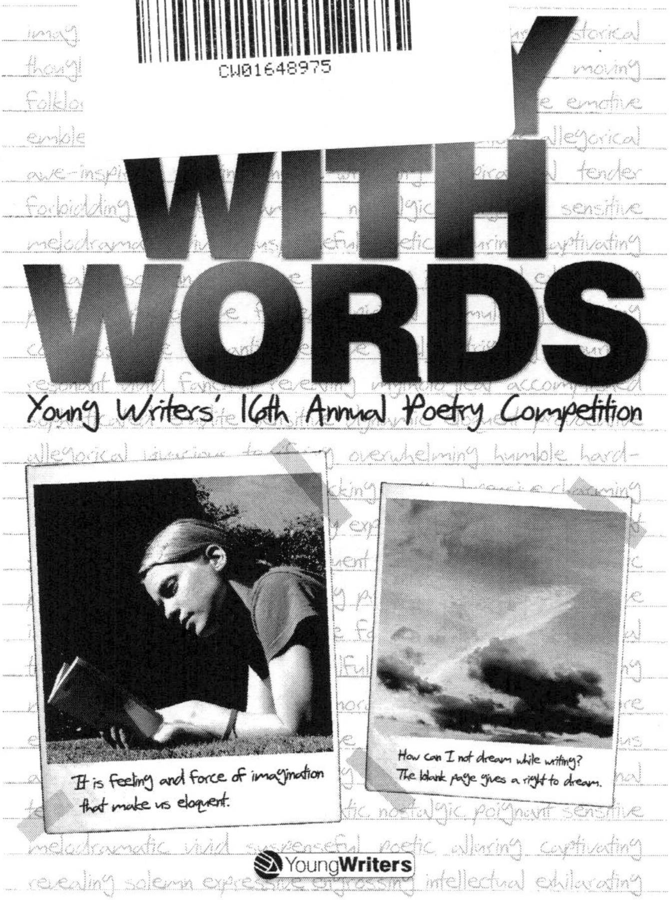

North East England

Edited by Donna Samworth

YoungWriters
First published in Great Britain in 2007 by:
Young Writers
Remus House
Coltsfoot Drive
Peterborough
PE2 9JX
Telephone: 01733 890066
Website: www.youngwriters.co.uk

SB ISBN 978-1 84431 236 8

Foreword

This year, the Young Writers' *Away With Words* competition proudly presents a showcase of the best poetic talent selected from thousands of up-and-coming writers nationwide.

Young Writers was established in 1991 to promote the reading and writing of poetry within schools and to the young of today. Our books nurture and inspire confidence in the ability of young writers and provide a snapshot of poems written in schools and at home by budding poets of the future.

The thought, effort, imagination and hard work put into each poem impressed us all and the task of selecting poems was a difficult but nevertheless enjoyable experience.

We hope you are as pleased as we are with the final selection and that you and your family continue to be entertained with *Away With Words North East England* for many years to come.

Contents

Wolsingham Comprehensive School, Wolsingham

The Poems

Who Would I Be

If I could be anyone, who would I be?
I would be my own boss.
Doing what I want to do.
Going where I want to go.
I would want people to take me seriously.

They think I am a constant joker
But I do have important things to say.
I would change all the mistakes I've made
The times I looked foolish.
I would have listened more in school
Paid attention to good advice.

I wouldn't change my personality.
I wouldn't change my sense of humour.
I wouldn't change the great friends in my life.

I can't change the mistakes I made in the past
But I can prevent the ones I could make in the future.

Martin Wilson
Barbara Priestman School, Sunderland

The Dreaded School Day

I wake up in the morning
With a really bad head
And I feel like I'm dead
I'm drowning in my own slaver.

I sit up in bed and feel strange and dizzy
Like I have sat on a Waltzer
I fall into my wheelchair
And attempt to go into the living room.

The taxi arrives when I don't want it to
My prayers weren't answered
Suddenly I have a bad stomach
In the background I hear my sister muttering.

In the taxi I have a laugh with my mates
Taking the mick out of everybody
As if I'm perfect myself
But I do it anyway.

I arrive at school . . . sorry prison
I think to myself, *what is the charge?*
Why am I here?
I've been wrongly accused.

It's nearly the end of my sentence
It feels like it's been life
I come out of the automatic doors
And sniff up - ahh the smell of freedom!

Chris Jackson (17)
Barbara Priestman School, Sunderland

It's Not Fair!

It's not fair,
When people jump in the queue,
Pretending you're not there,
Invisible, insignificant,
Sorry but I am here.

It's not fair,
When people shout loud,
Thinking you can't understand,
Angry, hurt,
Sorry but I can hear.

If you think you're better than me,
Why don't you try to be me?
See how this makes you feel,
But remember how it makes you like me.

Declan Meakin (16)
Barbara Priestman School, Sunderland

My Holiday In Menorca

Holidays are fun,
All that playing in the sun,
On the plane I sit and dream,
About the lollies and ice cream,
Swimming in the swimming pool,
Makes me feel nice and cool
Building sandcastles in the sand
Listening to my favourite band.

Helen Binns (17)
Barbara Priestman School, Sunderland

Rocco

Oh to have a puppy,
Is what I've dreamt about,
Today's the day my dream came true,
It made me scream and shout.

I love it when he barks and plays,
He really is such fun,
Rocco made me very happy,
He is my number one!

Michael Wright (16)
Barbara Priestman School, Sunderland

Exam Time

All the frustrations of the day
Explode in my face
My family don't think it is fair
They don't understand why I'm shouting
Being stuck in a classroom all day
No windows, no air
I don't think it is fair
That everyone is having fun but me
Exams make me scared
Isolated - no one to talk to
My mind goes blank
Just want to get it over with
So I can escape
No more school!

Glen Hutchinson (19)
Barbara Priestman School, Sunderland

It's Unfair

It's unfair
Do people not care?
It's unfair
I'm in a wheelchair!
I have not much independence outside
On my own I cannot ride
Disabled toilets make me frown
When they're locked it gets me down.
Most of them need a key
It's frustrating when I need a pee!
Just because people are unaware,
Doesn't mean they don't care,
I'm always self-conscious when I'm out
When people stare
I want to give them a clout
I don't mind when lasses stare at me
I'm really handsome as you can see.
So I know that life is unfair
But look at Third World countries, it's worse there.

Martin Wylie (17)
Barbara Priestman School, Sunderland

Turning Back Time

20!
Only 20
Never going to be a dad
Never going to see my mates again
No more fantastic views of the countryside
No more chats with my family
I am on the edge of the world
My life is coming to an end
All the things I wished I'd done
Flash before my eyes
Bungee-jumping from the clouds
Parachuting from a plane
More time
I need more time
I clutch my mam's hand
I whisper, 'I love you.'

Ash Boiston (17)
Barbara Priestman School, Sunderland

Pain

I have been through so much pain in my life
But I never complain
I just think of all my friends
Who are worse off than me
I have been through so much
I just feel like giving up
Sometimes life gets tough
But I put on a brave face.

But whatever comes my way
I know I can take it
With a little help from my mates
I will never give up!

Melissa Gibson (16)
Barbara Priestman School, Sunderland

My Life

Where can I begin?
My name is Margaret
I have blue eyes and blonde hair
I am a typical girly girl
But with a difference
I am 18 and in a wheelchair
Sometimes the wheelchair gets me down
It restricts me from being one of the gang
I would love to run into the sea
And feel sand between my toes
To walk up and down stairs
Instead of relying on a lift
To be able to look people in the eyes on their level
To be able to wear anything I like
To know I can jump on any bus
I know I am cared for
The best thing about my life
Are my friends at school
They all have problems and understand what I'm going through
But I long to be independent.

Margaret Christie (18)
Barbara Priestman School, Sunderland

A Poem About A Car

Bugati is a car
It goes very far
It is very fast
It never comes last
It is very small
So it never ever falls
It's got a lovely spoiler
And a small boiler
It's got brilliant wheels
So it never ever squeals
It's got a small door
Right next to the floor
It's got ten grills
So the water never fills
It's got a special gear stick
It's not even thick
It's got special seats
And room for your feet
It's a two seater
And hasn't got a meter.

Jordan Hackles (12)
Barbara Priestman School, Sunderland

What's Love Got To Do With It

Longing is a small flower waiting for love
Love is a feather floating from above
A fragile boat tossed about by emotion
Drifting away on the silky blue ocean

Romance is made with hearts and flowers
And a soft, sweet kiss until it sours
And hearts break into icy slivers of fears
Slivers into rivers into puddles of tears

Love turns crumbled hearts to stones
A gentle stick to break your bones.

Chris Ainsley (16) Sam Coulson (18) Jane Ducker (17)
Chelsea Keers (18) Sam Park (18) Adam Stoker (15)
Kirsty Stokes (18) & Mark Thackwray (15)
Catcote School, Hartlepool

Blue And Sunny

Blue and sunny
And calm air
Swallows gliding
Across the farmer's field
Looking for flies
You could see their
Shadows on the corn
It was beautiful.

Blue and sunny
And calm air
Me playing on
My trampoline
In the garden
My shadow on the grass
It felt like
I was flying
It was beautiful.

Gary Gair (14)
Cleaswell Hill School, Choppington

My Puppy

My puppy is scared of big dogs
She barks at them -
If they chase her
She runs into the house

I am scared of a big bully
She shouts at me
And chases me
I run into the house.

Vicky Malt (16)
Cleaswell Hill School, Choppington

Can You Guess What I Am?

Splits and spins
Cartwheels and handstands
Can you guess
What I am?
Outfits and pompoms too
High kicks in the air
Let's do
The high V
Low V
Broken T
Just T
Got any ideas now?
Left L Right L
1 2 3 4
My name is Maria
And I say, 'Hi'
5 6 7 8
Backing up and be my friend
I'm a cheerleader.

Maria Marchetti (14)
Cleaswell Hill School, Choppington

Steam Engine

We went to see a steam engine
You don't see an engine like that any more
It had shiny green paint
And the light on the front was bright
There were twelve carriages
And a lot of big wheels
The smell of the smoke was everywhere
After a while the engine
Had to go back to Newcastle
For a meal of coal and water
We took photographs
To remind us of
This powerful creature.

George Perkins (15)
Cleaswell Hill School, Choppington

What It's All About

I wandered through a woodland,
And pondered on this thought:
Amidst this life, where truly lay
The meaning that all sought?

Could it be found in leisure,
Or having fun with friends
Or maybe putting work aside
For playing? It depends.

Perhaps one finds fulfilment
In selfishness and pride.
In being first, in being best,
Whilst charity you hide.

Or finally, endeavouring
For riches, also fame.
The more you have, the more you want -
Yet is this really gain?

In going through that woodland,
The answer came to me:
In helping, guiding, loving others,
Happiest you'll be.

A smile lingered on my lips,
As softly fingered I
The rounded acorns of the trees
That on my palm did lie.

I thought, if one could sow the seeds
Of love in someone's heart,
In time that one would grow up kind
And loving, very smart,

And so I sought immediately
My sowing to begin.
Who knows? This very day I could
Sow seeds of love within.

Anna Winch (13)
Emmanuel College, Gateshead

Sunrise Passing

Peach clouds lay a natural carpet
Their curved peaks highlighted with a subtle pink,
The most pure sunrise.
The silence is broken with the cry of birds
And giant eagles fly past my eyes.

Feathers float in the warm currents of air
And suddenly the light catches white robes,
There are men and women riding these beasts.

I follow them to their destination,
And down a corridor of clouds,
An enormous gate that made the eagles
Look like sparrows and the people like ants.

The gate was pure gold inlaid with pearl
It opened,
I woke up,
Was this an image of Heaven?
I couldn't say
It was a heavenly sight, no matter what it was.

Douglas Garry (13)
Emmanuel College, Gateshead

That's Life

Taking the very first steps in life
The beginning of a unique journey in the beautiful world we share
Full of friends and foes
Sweet laughter and woes
A thrilling roller coaster of emotions
With ups and downs
Smiles and frowns
That's life.

And despite the occasional feeling of loneliness and sorrow
We know in our hearts
That there will always be tomorrow
A brand new day, a fresh new start
That holds unimaginable happenings
New faces, new voices
A whole variety of things
Oh, the joy and surprises life brings!
That's life.

But what is the meaning of life?
Surely we were put on the Earth for a reason?
To love, to have faith, to gain wisdom and teach others?
To enjoy our life as much as possible?
After all, we only have one chance to make a difference
One love
One world
One life
That's life.

Laura Scott (13)
Emmanuel College, Gateshead

The Mind Of A Madman

It's the mind of a madman,
That makes you like a dead man
And in here, if you are bad,
Darth Vader must be your dad!
And don't you even dare
Touch that man's facial hair,
Because Knuckles has washed his hands
And now there's blood everywhere!

The planet's intensifying,
With tribbles multiplying
And I am so, so hot
No wonder I have girls shot!
And the Teletubbies scream
At the truck of ice cream
And they didn't expect themselves
To get hit by a laser beam!

Sonic beats Mario to death
And here's the real Macbeth.
When the Borg fights the Daleks
Who has the Doctor and the Tardis!
Then Bin Laden gets bombed
By Secret Agent James Bond.
No wonder there's the fact
That Hitler is getting conned!

And much to my surprise . . .
Here's Captain Jean-Luc Picard
Of the USS Enterprise!

Andrew Dobson (15)
Glendene School, Peterlee

A World Through A Kid's Eyes

A world through a kid's eyes is big and new
Thinking about all of the new things you have to do
Like riding a bike and all of the other things you like to do
Like trying to have a good night's sleep
And waking up in the morning wide awake
Ready to start
A new day.

Daniel Howie (13)
Hylton Red House School, Sunderland

The Youth Of Today

Some teenagers carry knives
Some just try to live a normal life
Some teenagers live on drugs
Some of them are thugs
Some teenagers carry guns
Some just live with their mums
Some teenagers hang about in gangs
Most of them talk slang
Some teenagers are canny
Some teenagers scare grannies
Some teenagers are strong
Some of them have a pong
Don't take drugs
It's for mugs
Some teenagers smoke
But it's a joke.

Adam Gibson (12)
Hylton Red House School, Sunderland

If Only

If only I could turn back time,
That would be amazing,
I could be a Roman or a Viking finding new land,
Egyptian princess with bangles of gold,
Henry VIII's wife or maybe not,
Grace Kelly, Marylyn Monroe, someone like Audrey Hepburn
So beautiful,
If only, if only, if only
I could turn back time.

Megan Stevenson (13)
Hylton Red House School, Sunderland

The Dance

She's getting ready
For her big debut
The crowd goes silent
And the lights go blue
She takes to the stage
In a lovely tutu
She bows to the crowd
And does a perfect twirl
Then a man runs on
Looking desperate to win
He takes her hand and lifts her up
The crowd claps
Till their hands go rough
He puts her down
Takes a bow
It's up to the judges
What happens now?

Robyn Lister (12)
Hylton Red House School, Sunderland

You And Me

I look outside my window
And all I can see
Are many people
Just like you and me.

No matter what colour
Black or white
We get on so well
We never seem to fight.

I look outside my window
And all I can see
Are many people
Just like you and me.

We say hello
We say goodbye
But let me tell you
Our friendship will never die.

I look outside my window
And all I can see
Are many people
Just like you and me.

We walk, we talk
We dance, we sing
We always get on
Through thick and thin.

I look outside my window
And all I can see
Are many people
Just like you and me.

Michael Jones (13)
Hylton Red House School, Sunderland

The World Through The Eyes Of A Soldier

Another day away from home
On the front line defending all.
I like to think that I am doing my best,
By fighting for my country.
During this terrible World War I.

I receive a letter from my mother,
But my letters are always censored back.
She tells me how proud she is of me,
And that the Government uses a lot of
Propaganda to make young men join up.

I know that I am fighting to save my family and country,
I hope that I will soon be home.

Stacey Burn (15)
Hylton Red House School, Sunderland

My Voice

Ever since the day I was born
I have wondered how it would be,
To have a voice, to be able to talk
So people could hear me.

I can never share my feelings,
I get angry all the time,
It's as if me not being able to talk
Is always such a crime.

I wish people could hear me
So I can tell them how I feel
But instead I have to sit and wonder
And not make a great big deal.

I just wish I knew what it was like
To actually be able to talk
It's like not being able to read and write
Or even being able to walk.

But I suppose I will never know
I will be like this forever,
All my thoughts and feelings,
Will not get told . . . ever!

Jade Davis (11)
Hylton Red House School, Sunderland

Look At The World

If I looked through someone's eyes
I would see the world's not meant to be.

If I looked through someone's eyes
I would see the world doesn't revolve around me.

If I looked through someone's eyes
I would see the poor people next to me.

If I looked through someone's eyes
I would see the people fighting for their country.

If I looked through someone's eyes
I would see the people dying near.

If I looked through someone's eyes
I would see that their mams are never here.

Only if I could look through someone's eyes.

David Nicholls (14)
Hylton Red House School, Sunderland

Look At The World Through Someone Else's Eyes - An African Child

Why do we have no food?
But we are always still in a joyful mood
We always have to suffer in pain
Why can't we get a bit of grain?

Help me, help me, help me please
Will you if I beg on my knees?
We only have a little water
Help me to stop this horrible slaughter.

Little children standing crying
Because their mum is lying there dying
My little brother is only one
He still doesn't know what's going on.

I am sitting here with my feet tapping
Wondering what is going to happen
My mum's heart has stopped beating,
She is now in God's heavenly meeting.

Help me, help me, help me please
Will you if I beg on my knees?

Stephanie Sherry (14)
Hylton Red House School, Sunderland

Bullying

I look in the mirror and what do I see?
I think to myself *is that actually me?*
What have I turned into? What have I done?
I thought bullying was just for fun.
I can't make them run for the rest of the life
I guess I should give away my sharp shiny knife
But why do I have to put them in shame.
Make them go through all this pain?
What's the answer all to this?
I'll give that question one big miss.
I shake them around until they fizz
That's all I do, that's all it is.
But why can't I see who they are?
Maybe I can't travel that far.
Maybe they all have a heart of gold
Well that's what people have been told.
So I think I should stop and make a change
Make their life better instead of strange.
So I will stop this horrid pain
And move onto a better game.

Gina Thompson (13)
Hylton Red House School, Sunderland

Give A Voice To Someone Who Can't Speak - Bullying

Bullies hit and hurt
People think they are dirt
People are scared and cry
Bullies make people shy.

Bullies hurt and call
Bullies hurt the people who are small
People are scared
Now have lost the memories they shared.

People are laughing and joking
People hate the ones who are smoking
Bullies don't care and mind
They hurt the people inside.

Bullies think it's a joke
They splash water to get them soaked
Bullies laugh and think they're great
They bully people that have no mates.

Aimee Gordon (14)
Hylton Red House School, Sunderland

The World

If I could look at the world through someone else's eyes
I would see how difficult life could be.

If I could look at the world through someone else's eyes
I would realise that the world doesn't run around me.

I can't look at the world through someone else's eyes
So I will have to wonder what different people see.

George Udale (14)
Hylton Red House School, Sunderland

Press Stop Bugging Teens

The youth of today
All of them are bad the press say
Don't take drugs
Or set fire to rugs
They don't break windows for fun
Don't shoot people with a gun
The press reckon we're all bad
And they are really driving us mad
You'd think we've robbed a bank
Or even blown something up with a tank
All we want to do is have some fun
When we see the press we run
If they catch us they will ask us a question
And will demand an explanation
The question will be, 'What's it like to be a teen?'
We will just say, 'You are very mean.'
The press say we have a lot of fights
But we are sure they've violated our rights
We will tell the press to stop acting like a baby
Then we will answer your questions, maybe.

Liam Conoly (14)
Hylton Red House School, Sunderland

Poor Madeleine

People are so sad,
That a little girl,
Has been took by a big horrible human,
Her parents are worried and petrified,
Her twins are crying,
With worry and fright,
Her life is not over,
She has still got years left,
Is she still alive?
Just hope for the best,
And she will come home tonight,
The humans who has kidnapped her,
Should be ashamed of themselves,
They have took a lovely beautiful,
Girl away from a loving family,
It has been on the news
That people have put £2.5 million
To save poor Madeline,
We hope for the best,
That she comes back safely,
To her heartbroken family.

Jaye Skinner (12)
Hylton Red House School, Sunderland

The Unfortunate

I feel so lucky with a roof over my head
Then I look at people who have to beg
Eating scraps and drinking them too
I hope that has not happened to you.

I stand and stare, how sad
I hope it's not that bad
Poor little lad.

I wish I could help them, yes I do
I would give them food and good clothes too,
I wish they could live a life like me and you.

Please help the homeless.

Amy Leadbitter (12)
Hylton Red House School, Sunderland

Murder

I murdered someone
Now she is gone,
I feel guilt in my heart,
Her heart, I took apart,
I wonder, will they find out,
Damn, I heard her shout,
I'm going to get put in jail,
I killed her, I went pale,
It was an accident,
Ah, I wish I was Superman/Clarke Kent,
To fly away,
One day I promise I will pay,
I got annoyed, I'm sorry,
Ahh, I pushed her in front of a lorry,
Before that I stabbed her,
With a knife,
Do you know that 'she?'
It was my wife!

James Redford (12)
Hylton Red House School, Sunderland

Why Are We Here?

Why are we here?
I mean you no harm,
Because we could be animals
Running around on a farm.

We could be dead,
Or have a disease,
So answer my question,
I'm down on my knees.

There are people dying
With no water or food,
They just sit there thinking
Why am I here?

I could be somewhere
Where I have friends to hold
Not sitting here thinking and suffering,
In the freezing cold.

I have sleepless nights,
Trying to figure it out,
Trying to rack my brains
What is it really about?

So help me on this one
I'm stricken by fear
I'm desperately asking
Why are we here?

Steffanie Ward (14)
Hylton Red House School, Sunderland

People!

People think they are so cool
People think they are hip hop,
People think they are really popular,
But they are really not.

People think they are so good looking,
People put make-up on their faces,
People think they are the best,
But they are really not.

People think they should do everything they say,
People boss them about,
People do everything they tell them,
But really they should not.

People think they can get away with things,
People tell people to do their dirty work,
But really they should not.

People are really kind,
People are really funny,
People make you laugh,
But they really should do.

Shawni Unsworth (12)
Hylton Red House School, Sunderland

Gears

Marcus Fenix you're the leader
You figured out how to kill a seeder.
Dom you're the brains of the lot
You know what to do when the going gets hot.
There's only one big man that's Cole,
Enemies lose you when you do a side roll.
Baird, Baird, what would they do
Without you, it's nowhere near a crew?
Kim you were the one
But Raam came and now you're gone.
Hoffman you're the big boss
You sent in Kim and that was your loss.
Carmine you were so cool
But your head went, what a fool.
Raam why were you bad?
You had a nice gun Gatlin, that's what you had.
Now here I am and all I need to say is,
Thanks to those Gears who saved the day.

Jack Potts (11)
Hylton Red House School, Sunderland

Madeleine

Poor Maddie's Mum and Dad,
They must be very sad,
The little girl got taken away
Whilst they were on their holiday.

Taking children is a crime,
Your whole life to do the time,
The person who finds her is one in a billion,
The reward is a huge £2.5 million.

Little Maddie can still be found,
The Portuguese police should look around,
If she's found we won't be sad,
The little twins will be really glad.

Declan Burdis (11)
Hylton Red House School, Sunderland

Madeleine

She has gone
The oldest one
It's broken my heart
That we are apart.

Will they attack
And will she come back?
I miss her that much
There's no one else as such.

Was I right
Or was I wrong?
Was I right
To leave her alone?

It's been so long,
For the time she's been gone
Will they put up a fight,
Now she's out of my sight?

Jodie Halliday (11)
Hylton Red House School, Sunderland

Madeleine

Maddie's mam is very sad,
Maddie's dad is very bad,
Maddie's friends hope she's alright
Because she's out of her mam and dad's sight,
She's only four years old,
And very small,
The people who took her must be very tall.
Maddie's our little princess,
The people who took her haven't been through the court test,
They did the crime,
They should do the time.

Caitlan Anderson (12)
Hylton Red House School, Sunderland

Madeleine

Madeleine has been taken
She has to waken,
She's a poor little girl,
She is in one big whirl,
Her mam and dad are very worried.

All of her family are very sad
The people who took her are very glad,
We don't know where she is,
Or what she is doing,
Now her family's life is ruined.

She must be very mixed up,
I bet she doesn't even drink out of a cup,
Our poor Maddie
She's not even the baddie.

Demi Cooper (11)
Hylton Red House School, Sunderland

All The Poor!

Think of all those refugees and others,
No parents to hug or love.
Try and put yourself in them,
No home to live or keep warm.
Think of them, what would they say?
No food that me and you eat.
Cold in winter with no blankets,
No money to buy them either.

Sarah Cairns (12)
Hylton Red House School, Sunderland

Madeleine

Madeleine please come back,
I don't want you dead in a sack,
I will always see you through,
I will make it up to you,
People who took you didn't care,
About your blue eyes and blonde hair,
You mean everything to me,
I wish people could see,
How I suffer every night,
To not have Madeleine in sight.

Liam Goldsmith (12)
Hylton Red House School, Sunderland

Madeleine

Madeleine's been took from all our love
They must be sick and horrible men
Pray have faith in our Lord above
We will see Madeleine again
Maybe in spirit or maybe in whole
She's been gone a while with no sound
With all the police on patrol
But I bet she'll stand her ground.

Her mam and dad in sorrow for what these men have done
Madeleine doesn't deserve this
It's not a joke, neither is it fun
But she is till in God's kiss
Let faith be with us all
Let Madeleine stand tall!

Jamie Lister (12)
Hylton Red House School, Sunderland

At Home

In the corner all alone
Up against the solid stone
Standing up for all my rights
Always getting into fights
Wishing I had just one friend
Or if my life should just end
Sitting there all the time
It is such a horrible crime.

Daddy is a real bad man
He hits me with a frying pan
I scream and I cry
To the teachers I have to lie
He killed my mum and sister too
Maybe he will come get you
He told police it was suicide
Little did they know he had just lied.

Calvin Hope (12)
Hylton Red House School, Sunderland

The Beast

Horrid and ugly and very bad,
Bubbling and boiling it's very mad.
A stupid thing never before seen,
It's got loads of spots like a teen.

Coming after me faster and faster,
It was like a total disaster.
I ran and ran as fast as I could,
If you were me you know you would.

It was really catching up to me,
I'm not a very good runner you see.
Then all of a sudden I fell,
I couldn't get up, I knew, I could tell.

I closed my eyes by pure fear,
I thought I nearly shed a tear.
I opened my eyes to see a big blister,
Oh! Phew! It's just my sister.

Callum Veitch (12)
Hylton Red House School, Sunderland

Bubbles

Bubbles, bubbles all around
Bubbles, bubbles they make a sound
Bubbles, bubbles I wonder why
Bubbles, bubbles go so high.

Bubbles, bubbles big and small
Bubbles, bubbles tiny and tall
Bubbles, bubbles black and blue
Bubbles, bubbles are so cool.

Hayley Matthews (12)
Hylton Red House School, Sunderland

My Family

My family are the strangest,
The strangest they can be.
My dad in an elephant suit
He likes to embarrass me.

My sister loves sandcastles,
She's a sandcastle at heart.
It makes me giggle, it makes me laugh,
When she makes a man and a cart.

My uncle is Formula One mad,
But that's not really all.
He likes the circus, all that stuff
Especially stilts that make him tall.

My cousin likes pink bunnies too,
She's really, really crazy.
It's really funny, it's really daft
When she acts like a daisy.

My mam is a footy fanatic
And you'd say what's strange about that.
You wouldn't really be saying so
If you knew she brings the cat.

Then there's me, the average one
Who is extremely clever.
And here I am, a poet at large
And nothing to rhyme with clever.

Alanna Hudson (12)
Hylton Red House School, Sunderland

Hylton Red House

From Mrs Quincey
To the cleaners
From Mr Brady
To Mr Ramsden
HRH is the best.

From Mrs Miller
To all of us
From Mrs Compton
To Mr Kernen
HRH is the best.

From the teachers
To the workmen
And finally from the school itself
To everyone in it
HRH is the best!

Gary Ewart (12)
Hylton Red House School, Sunderland

Landmarks Of Sunderland

Walking past the Stadium of Light
I can feel the Sunderland players' might
When I walk up Penshaw Hill
The height gives me a chill.

I have fun at Downhill Park
You could go to the beach to look for a shark.
I love to see the park of Herrington
Let's read on for I'm not done.

Hylton Castle is a great place to be
Keep on looking there's more to see.
Yes, Sunderland is a really great place
Recommended to all of the human race.

Matthew Beckett (11)
Hylton Red House School, Sunderland

My Grandad James

My grandad was called James
And he was very kind.
Now he has gone
But he's always on my mind.

He always loved his garden
He was in it all the time.
He would always sit and watch
The fabulous sunshine.

He would take me everywhere.
I can always remember the good times I had.
Now that my grandad James is gone
I am really, really sad.

Jessica Letson (12)
Hylton Red House School, Sunderland

The Jackson Family

There's a brother, his name is Tom.
He was digging in the garden when he found a bomb.
Their mam was in the kitchen making tea
While Charlotte played with a bee.
David was reading the dictionary
Their aunt and uncle played Pictionary.
Kelly was on the phone to a boy
Then Sophie tossed a toy.
The bomb was fully loaded
That's when it exploded.

Fiona Mullen (11)
Hylton Red House School, Sunderland

Bullying

They rip my tie, rip my shirt.
They haven't a clue that I'm hurt.
I've only one friend and one only,
It's my bestest friend and her name's Toni.
Gangs of bullies walk ahead,
I wish the day was over or I'd stayed in bed.
They call, kick me, spit as well.
They tripped me up and over I fell.
I told my mam, she phoned the school.
It gets worse, they try to drown me in the pool.
After all, I've got my friend
I will stick with her until the end.

Shawnee Lay (13)
Hylton Red House School, Sunderland

Balances

The balances of life
Are not settled with a knife.
It's all about
How we treat each other.
We can be happy.
We can be sad.
We can be angry.
Our friends mean a lot
Even when they've lost the plot.
But we'll always be there
For each other.

Kirstin Nicholson (13)
Hylton Red House School, Sunderland

Sunderland

We are going to the Premiership.
Say goodbye to the Championship.
Bring on Newcastle
We will beat them with no hassle.
The FA Cup is coming back
Fighting spirit we don't lack.
The Sunderland team will keep on fighting.
Carlos Edwards is as fast as lightning.

Stephen Jackson (12)
Hylton Red House School, Sunderland

Life

Life is good, life is bad.
Life is happy, life is sad.
One minute you're relaxing cutting your lawn,
The next thing you know your baby's been born.
Your life's going well, then you take a stumble,
The life around you starts to crumble.
You go on silent, walking miles each day.
But there's nowhere else for you to stay.
Then, when the time's right, you start to fade,
Only your child to watch you get laid.
In peace of Hell you struggle to lie,
You wonder and cry to know why.
You died happy accompanied by a knife.
Bumpy, happy and unknown in your life.
Life is good, life is bad.
Life is happy. But your life's sad.
In Heaven you rest.

Paige Neale (12)
Hylton Red House School, Sunderland

Dying

Giggles, screams and angry cries,
A guilty dream packed with lies.
A hurting child lost and alone
Listening to his mother moan.
Her dreams are dying
An empty heart crying.
They cuddle up and forget their lies
And wait for the time they say . . .
Goodbye.

Larissa Banks (13)
Hylton Red House School, Sunderland

Our Community

I look outside in the big bad community
It looks like everyone has an immunity
Gas and fumes all around
As I look up on the great big mound.

Hounds are always chasing me
Why can't they just leave me be?
People always getting into fights
What about their human rights?

I dare not look behind
As kidnappers and rapists play with my mind
Metal objects whizzing past my head
I just can't wait to go to bed.

As bullets ricochet off my wall
I wonder why can't it be normal and play football
As I look through the eyes of our community
Not everyone can have an immunity.

Craig Newby (13)
Hylton Red House School, Sunderland

Turn Back Time What Would You Change?

If I could turn back time
I would make all the people shine
No one would have to cry
Then no one would be shy.

If people were ill
Well they won't be still
There will be fun
And you won't have to run.

There will be no hitting,
Then the children will be sitting
There will be no starvation
Then the world will be a better nation.

I would change the bullies
And make sure they don't wear hoodies,
I won't have to think is that my name?
Is my life just a game?

Kirsty Morris (13)
Hylton Red House School, Sunderland

I Cannot Speak

My eyes are sore
My legs are weak
I cannot even get to sleep.
For all the lies and deceit
Why can't I be my little brother Pete?

My face is scarred,
And my hands are cut
How they make me crawl through muck.
I'm forced to sleep, with no bed,
In the garden, in the shed.

I'm so cold, I cannot move
Just to prove to Mum and Dad
They have treated me so bad.

My ribs are bruised
I'm covered in blood
The shed is like . . .
The tsunami flood.

I close my eyes, and curl up tight
Thinking this is my last night.
I cannot cry and show my fear
This is the very last time I hear.

These words are repeated in my head,
In the morning I'm left for dead.

Rebecca Stoker (14)
Hylton Red House School, Sunderland

Childhood Memories

Good times, great memories
Are when you are a baby
Taking your first step
To eating proper meals.

Saying your first word, I give it a go
No one will laugh,
No one will joke,
Give it a go, no one will choke.

You are small and cuddly
You light up my day
When I see you my troubles go away.

Till we get teenagers, we are little terrors
But not all teenagers are bad.
The youth of today, shake off stereotype
Put your side across
Teenagers are teenagers.

We meant to bully, we meant to harm?
That's not what teenagers are like
Teenagers do good things
Teenagers can do bad things
But that's not what teenagers are like
We're meant to shout
We're meant to scream
That's what teenagers do.

We're meant to fight
We're meant to argue
That's what teenagers do.

Teenagers are not terrors
Teenagers are just teenagers
So let them live their lives
Don't give them a fright.

Gemma Willis (14)
Hylton Red House School, Sunderland

What Would It Be Like

What would it be like
If I could speak up,
What would it be like,
If life revolved around me?
What would it be like to be such a thing?
What would it be like if I spoke for myself?
Maybe I could reach a mountain
In a few small steps,
What would it be like
If everyone evolved around me?
I wish I could stand up and speak up
But I can't,
I just sliver in the corner,
Like a coward,
And do nothing,
What would it be like,
If the world was this way?

Liam Brook (14)
Hylton Red House School, Sunderland

Vanished Angel

We are doing the best we can
Looking for Madeleine McCann.
The Portuguese police make arrests
The British police have a few suspects.
In Rotherly friends are sad,
Worried are her mum and dad.
As we look high and low
Time to stop no, no, no, no, no, no!
As we keep a picture of her in our heads
There is bad news that the families dread.

Alex Connor (12)
Hylton Red House School, Sunderland

I Wonder?

I wonder why the sky is so high
I wonder why we like to sigh
I wonder why the ground is so low
I wonder why we wear a bow.

I wonder why we eat pie
I wonder why people wear a tie
I wonder why we have a beach
I wonder why we have a leech.

I wonder why we have rain
I wonder why we use a lane
I wonder why we have a telly
I wonder why we wear a welly.

I wonder why we have the sea
I wonder why we have the name Lee
I wonder why we have a poster
I wonder why we make a toaster.

Charlotte Sawczyn (12)
Hylton Red House School, Sunderland

Turn Back Time

If I could turn back time,
What would I change?

I would change
Old people getting hurt,
Getting named,
Getting hit as some may have fits.

If I could turn back time,
What would I change?

I would change
Families fighting,
Families biting,
While children have to watch.
What if they were tots?

If I could turn back time,
What would I change?

I would change
Country starvation,
What happens in time,
Bless non have done a crime.

Why is this?
We all say,
Time changes every day.

Dionne Robins (14)
Hylton Red House School, Sunderland

A Bully Can Be . . .

A bully can be short,
A bully can be tall,
A bully can be strong,
A bully can be small,
A bully can be cruel,
A bully can be a teen,
A bully can be popular,
A bully can be keen,
A bully can force you to run or hide away,
A bully can be someone you see in the mirror every day.

Chelsea Thompson (12)
Hylton Red House School, Sunderland

Luck

Luck is a thing
What everyone's got,
Luck makes you happy,
Even when you're not.
Luck can be bad, worse than you think,
People getting promoted,
Others losing their jobs,
Buying a new house,
Others on the street,
Buying food to last for years,
While others starve.

Sarah Usher (12)
Hylton Red House School, Sunderland

Madeleine

Maddi went missing 12 days ago,
Only at the age of four,
She has blue eyes
And blonde hair,
The people who took her didn't care,
She'll be all alone,
Nowhere to stay,
Sitting with the people who took her away,
Her mum and dad have a bad head,
Thinking that she is dead,
Her family and friends, hope she's OK
And that she'll come home one day.

Amy McCririe (12)
Hylton Red House School, Sunderland

My Last Goodbye

I'm sitting here all alone
Clinging to my telephone.
What can I do?
Just sit here trembling all night long,
For what he's done I know is wrong.
If I dial, what do I say?
For then I need to run away.

He's coming for me,
Why can't I see?
He said when he finds me it's my turn to die,
So this, my friend, is my last goodbye.

Lauren Waites (12)
Hylton Red House School, Sunderland

Unspoken Romance

I stood in the corridor,
Watching as you smiled.

My heart pounded,
What do I do?
Every time I see you,
My heart goes boom, boom.

I know you don't see me,
The way I see you,
Maybe if you knew me,
You'll feel this way too.

This would never be said,
By a girl truly in love,
Because she is too shy,
And doesn't want to face
    Rejection.

Hannah Watson (13)
Hylton Red House School, Sunderland

Why Are We Here?

The world would be so boring
if we weren't here
The world would be so boring
if children weren't here to have fun
The world would be so boring
if there were no colourful flowers
The world would be so boring
if there were no animals
The world would be so boring
if there were no parks.

Lucy Varley (12)
Hylton Red House School, Sunderland

The Past

Would you turn back time if you could?
Would you do the thing you always should?
It's good to be where we are in life
Wait and see, I'll prove you right.

See your ancestors, see the past
Come with me I'll take you back
We're in the past, hip hip hooray
You can say the things you couldn't say.

This is the end of my journey back
I'll go to the future
But I'll be back.

Luke Thompson (11)
Hylton Red House School, Sunderland

Indian Tiger

Pounces and stalks a bird
Strolls along the leaves and dirt
Her paws thump as they hit the ground
A day in the Indian Savannah
Her golden coat and marvellous stripes gleam in the sun
Looks and feels her cubs
She sleeps under the Indian sunset.
She is the queen of the plains of India
The symbol of beauty
She moves like a ball of fire
A marvellous majestic species
Please don't let it disappear.

Ellie Burrell (12)
Hylton Red House School, Sunderland

Through The Eyes Of Paul Collingwood

Diving to my left,
At backward point,
I take the catch,
See ya Ponting.

I'm the 4th seamer,
Thundering into bowl,
Off stumps out the ground,
Bye bye Gilchrist.

With my 2nd delivery,
I dismiss Hussey,
That's 2 in 2,
I'm on a hat-trick.

With my 3rd bowl,
Clarke gets an edge,
Prior to his left,
What a fantastic catch.

Now I'm in bat,
200 to win,
Me and Flintoff,
Brilliant partners.

Bracken runs in,
On the off stump,
I hit it out the ground,
That's my century and we win . . .
The Ashes.

Sean Atkinson (11)
Lord Lawson of Beamish School, Birtley

Through The Eyes Of . . . Britney Spears

All I want is a friend to trust,
Why are they so hard to find?
I always feel like I must,
Find a way of letting out the hurt inside.
They always treat me differently,
Because I shaved my head,
Because I've suffered from depression,
Since my divorce from K-Fed.
He was the one who ruined me,
The one who made me ill,
Sometimes I even ended up,
Resorting to the pill.
My parents are supportive,
My sister and children too,
They always treat me very well,
Someday I hope you will too.
I used to party all night,
Until the sun came up,
I finally got so ill that,
I decided to give it up.
I went into rehab,
To get help and find a friend,
Now I've got a good one,
My life is on the mend.

Kelly Baldwin (11)
Lord Lawson of Beamish School, Birtley

Through The Eyes Of The Queen

I threw on my robes,
And slipped on my crown,
I climbed into the carriage,
Where it all began.

I was taken on a journey,
To the Coronation,
I arrived on time,
For the celebration.

I heard a tiger's roar,
Coming from the crowd,
First I was astonished,
Then I curtsied and bowed.

I watched the band,
Marching down the street,
While there were hands clapping,
And stamping from feet.

I walked slowly forward,
Meetings and greetings all around,
Was everyone here to see me?
They were making such a sound.

I felt so appreciated,
I felt so respected,
I felt so sophisticated,
I felt accepted.

Jennifer Beattie (12)
Lord Lawson of Beamish School, Birtley

Through The Eyes Of Kevin Pieterson

Yo I'm KP
That's my name,
I play cricket for England,
Cos I love the fame.

I love to hit the biggest six,
The cover drive for four.
Beware that fielder at mid off,
Cos you'll have to field some more.

Nice bowling Shane,
Well not for long.
Cos when I pick up my bat,
I'll cruise along.

My favourite shot is to sweep the ball,
Because I am so very tall.
I can hit the ball such a long, long way
Not even Collingwood would try and get in the way.

We English cricketers love success,
Nothing more, nothing less.
When we beat the Aussies, in one day cricket and test,
English cricket will be back to its best.

The Ashes in 2005,
Our winning hopes were very high.
Cos when me and Freddie came in to bat,
We were always ready, there's no doubt about that.

But the Ashes 2007
Aussies had their trophy back,
And after the World Cup in the Caribbean,
Our coach Duncan Fletcher got the sack.

But we'll soon be back!

Aidan Beck (12)
Lord Lawson of Beamish School, Birtley

Through The Eyes Of . . .

Such ugly things I've had to see,
So many places I've been forced to be,

Some people use me as a dangerous tool,
But they get arrested,
I pity the fool,

Some people use me to chop down trees,
But then they get splinters stuck in their knees,

I'm lethal and sharp,
And I puncture men's hearts,

I'm hard and I'm steel,
And I cut up car wheels,

I'm a knife as you can see,
And danger follows whoever wears me,

Why people keep me, I don't know,
But some people keep me just for show!

Ian Brewis (11)
Lord Lawson of Beamish School, Birtley

Campside Worry

I was lost on a campsite,
In the middle of the night,
My parents were lost,
They had gone for a shower,
Just for one hour.
They had left me and my sister,
In the tent,
My mam had sent
A message!
Just to remind
Us that just behind
Us was the car,
With the games in,
In a small round tin.
My parents would be back
In quarter of an hour,
They were leaving the shower,
My sister was worrying,
We wish they were hurrying,
We wish they would get back.

Andrew Brown (11)
Lord Lawson of Beamish School, Birtley

Through The Eyes Of . . . A Dog

Did I do something wrong?
My owner abandoned me,
What could it be?
Did I hurt him?
Or was it his new girlfriend Kim?

A van drove by,
I heard a massive sigh,
They stopped,
They picked me up,
'He's only a pup!'

They took me to a shelter,
The journey was a helter skelter,
Next day someone bought me,
She took me to her home,
Now every day she gives me a bone.

She walks me and feeds me,
Gives me drinks and squeaky toys,
Her other dog gives me lots of love,
She's not at all rough,
I love my new owner.

My life is almost over,
I've had good times,
I've had bad times,
My life is coming to an end,
Say goodbye to all my friends!

Rebecca Carver (12)
Lord Lawson of Beamish School, Birtley

Through The Eyes Of Belle

Here I am,
I am Belle,
Under the table,
I see Hell,

The men walk in,
I've never seen them before.
They shout and yell,
The words I hear them roar.

Comes the dog,
I hear him cry.
The men bash about,
Do I see him die?

Mummy comes,
I see her feet,
The men they curse and Mummy's screams
Can be heard in the street.

I'm not scared,
But Mummy is,
Here under the table,
I'm safe.

Soldiers they come here,
All the time.
My mummy cries,
All the time,

I see the rain,
On the windowpane,
The men they leave for war,
And I'm happy again.

Where is Mummy?
She's under the table with me.

Charlotte Clark (12)
Lord Lawson of Beamish School, Birtley

Through The Eyes Of A Misunderstood Boy

Why do they think this?
What did I do wrong?
My family is dead,
So I'm the only one.

We weren't vampires at all,
Oh no, we were human.
I'm only fourteen years old,
So please understand me.

I have to hide away now,
It's just not fair!
Just because I live in the dark,
And have unusual hair.

Everyone is out to get me,
To make sure I'm dead.
They bring their stakes and crosses,
To make sure I'm pouring crimson red.

So along come these people,
All happy and bright,
Just talking to me,
Was a wonderful sight!

They said they would help me,
By putting their lives in danger!
And as they were planning,
Along came a ranger.

He fired his gun twice,
Knocking me down,
And so lay the boy,
With his blood-stained frown.

Georgia Duffy (12)
Lord Lawson of Beamish School, Birtley

Through The Eyes Of A Lost Orphan

I am lost in some place, somewhere
I don't know where to go
Lost on Christmas Eve
Out cold in the snow
I never knew my parents
Don't even know their names
Now I clutch a thin sheet
I stole from a stall in the high street
My brother looks at me hopefully
Wanting everything to be fine
But he doesn't know what fine is
We have always been this way
For as long as I can remember
Someone placed us on a street
She was young, I remember her some
Sometimes I wonder If she was my mum
My brother starts weeping
For it is so cold on his thin bones
Why does no one help us?
Does anyone care?
As the sun, our only friend
Shares the last of its light
My little sibling shudders
I only hope he survives tonight
I am his carer, to give him hope
Ever since he has been alive
Into the deep realms of sleep he dives
I am seven, and he is five.

Chris Hamilton (12)
Lord Lawson of Beamish School, Birtley

Through The Eyes Of A Football

I'm a football being whacked around,
They kick me before I even hit the ground.

Sometimes the goalkeeper makes a save,
But it doesn't matter cos I feel like a slave.

They don't seem to realise that I have feelings,
Even when my layers come off like peelings.

My red and black covering glints in the sun,
But I still can't seem to have any fun.

Even if I'm kicked off the right post,
They don't seem to think I'm as good as most.

Even if I hit the net,
I don't get the respect I really should get.

They think I'm just rubber and air,
Even if they burst me as a dare.

Even when I get booted
I'm never ever, ever hooted.

They send me round in a free kick
It feels like they're hitting me with a stick.

But it doesn't matter cos I'm just a ball,
I'll give a little scream before I hit the wall.

James Hayes (12)
Lord Lawson of Beamish School, Birtley

Meaning Of Life

All alone in the big brown bag,
It's scary, it's wicked, it's very sad.
I lie there and wonder why I am here,
But in the end I can't choose.

I am all stuffed up and it makes me hot,
It makes me something I am not.
How can I get away from this awful place but of course I can't,
I don't have a meaning in my life.

When my stitching comes away I cry inside,
And how much I wish I could be wide.
The pens and pencils all around,
But I can't pick them up because I'm a nobody.

My life is meaningless but I have to put up with it,
I wish I would die.
I can't because I have no freedom,
Because my life is meaningless.

Many people think a pencil case is just a piece of stationery,
But it's not so treat it with respect.

Jessica Leask (12)
Lord Lawson of Beamish School, Birtley

Through The Eyes Of Gerard Way

Wake up every day, I haven't really changed
I'm just richer and more famous than I was and everyone knows my name
I get fan mail, business mail and hate mail by the sack,
Saying things from how great you are to saying you should go break your back.

Go outside, walk the streets
See people you thought you'd never meet.
People point, shout and stare,
Forget you have feelings just like theirs.

Can't go out without being shouted abuse at
People have hit, kicked, punched and spat,
Just because I'm different, and stand out in a crowd,
I can't change who I am but I try to be proud.

I look in the mirror, I don't like what I see
Apparently people find me attractive but I'm just me.
People hate me but I hate myself more
Someday they'll find me lying dead on the floor.

Love my music, love my band
Love my family and all my fans
I'll die sometime but not today
I know who I am, I'm Gerard Way.

Emma Leyland (12)
Lord Lawson of Beamish School, Birtley

Through The Eyes Of A Schoolbag

The boy walks up; I'm lying on the floor, just like before.
My zip goes zip and I see him pour pens, pencils and rubbers into my jaw -
He picks me up and zips me up, walks down the street to a constant beat,
The school's in view, I hear a 'Phew!'
His friends are there, my friends too.
Each has a bag on their back, each held up by a single strap.
The school bell goes and I go too, carried off to a lesson in Room Two.
The kids sit down but I stay still, opened up and left to spill,
Out the pens and the rubbers
Chucked away, dumped on the ground
The ground beats fast to a mighty pound, as I lie lifeless on the ground.
The bell rings again and I'm thrust away
- this is my day!

Rhys Mantle (12)
Lord Lawson of Beamish School, Birtley

Through The Eyes Of A . . . School Jumper

Over the shoulder
Covered in hair
Tie underneath
Perfect to wear

I'm moving around
Then I stop
Walking up a hill
Past a garage shop

I'm at my destination
People crowd around
I notice more like me
Running on the ground

I hit the floor
My owner cries
Someone just hit her
Much bigger in size

How can I help it
It's happened before
My black and yellow colours
Lying on the floor.

Many things just like me
Have had it done as well
Red, green and blue too
Also can't help but dwell.

Back down the hill
Sitting down ever so still
Wondering, thinking
About what had happened
And if it would happen again.

Lauren Matthews (11)
Lord Lawson of Beamish School, Birtley

Through The Eyes Of . . .

I am a dangerous weapon,
And I am known as a criminal.
I love to go bang.

Whether it's 'stick em up'
Or 'stop or I'll shoot'
I'm always loaded for the job.

Close or long range,
I'm lethal in any
I can be cocked or shelled.

I'm used in robberies,
Or hostage holds,
Even the odd murder or more.

But one word of warning
If you ever use me
Whether you hit or not
You'll go down five years or more.

Nicky Mowbray (12)
Lord Lawson of Beamish School, Birtley

Misunderstood

Children and teenagers in these days,
Are misunderstood in many ways.
All they do is hang on the streets,
This makes them get in trouble with the police.

But under all that deep inside,
Is something they feel they have to hide.
Some time ago kids could play in the trees,
And run around freely.

But now that's called trespassing or breaking the law,
And once again kids would get called.
We want to have fun and run in the forests,
Or have our own secret cottage.

So can't everyone just listen,
Or can't they see there is something missing.
We just want to go out and run,
Because all we want is a little fun.

So bring this deep in thought,
And less of us will go to court.
And maybe they won't steal your car,
Because children and teenagers aren't what you think they are.

Abbie Stott (12)
Lord Lawson of Beamish School, Birtley

Turn Back Time To Kielder

If I could turn back time,
I would go to Kielder,
A favourite place of mine,
It was by a lake,
And it smelt like pine,
But we had a lot of fun.

The forest was the first stop,
Then we went orienteering,
We could only go so far because of a drop,
Then we went to a glass maze,
I was so tired it made me flop,
But we still stayed up until 10 o'clock

On the second day,
We made a shelter,
It was not somewhere that I wanted to stay,
We went for dinner and canoeing,
Down the lake all the way,
It made us very wet.

However we had a lot of sweets that night,
Now it was last day,
And we weren't feeling very bright,
We made plastic rockets,
They went an amazing height,
Finally I went on a jet ski.

If I could turn back time,
I would go to Kielder,
A favourite place of mine,
It was by a lake,
And it smelt like pine,
But we had a lot of fun.

Laura Taylor (12)
Lord Lawson of Beamish School, Birtley

Through The Eyes Of . . . Yao Ming

I wake up in the morning,
Hit my head off the roof,
I'm seven foot six and I
Can't get in a telephone booth.
I stand near the rim, slam the ball through the net,
I play every season cos I'm in debt.

When I'm chasing the ball down the court,
My calves are hurting and my arms feel like curtains
But I'm still one of the best.
I shoot for three
And then see
I'm only made for dunks.

I slam it and win it,
But I don't feel I'm with it
We win the game
Everyone's cheering 'Go Yao go Yao,'
That's what I'm hearing.

My jobs are done
Then I go home
I see my kid he's a little gnome.

Dean Astley (14)
Lord Lawson of Beamish School, Birtley

Through The Eyes Of . . . A Football

Through the eyes of a football
It is not very pleasant at all
All the time you get kicked all day
Off all the kids who want to play.

When they have finished I get stored away
And don't come out until they want to play
I get carried around in somebody's hand
Listening to the cheerleaders and the band.

I get kicked around all over the pitch
Hitting every bump and every ditch
I get squeezed and squashed for 90 minutes
Until the children have to go for their dinners.

I get trampled on by all those feet
Playing in all sorts of weather, even sleet
I get dirty and muddy every day
They treat me as if I'm a slave.

I'm always dirty I never get cleaned
If I had my way I would use Mr Sheen
I really wish somebody would clean me
Then I could be proud and smile with glee.

Through the eyes of a football
It is not very pleasant at all
All the time you get kicked all day
Off all the kids who want to play.

Adam Berry (14)
Lord Lawson of Beamish School, Birtley

Untitled

T ough life for a well-used bag like me?
H ow does one thing cope?
R eally stuffy and hot it is,
O n this little shopping trip,
U naccepting my plea for freedom,
G oing in and out digging for her phone,
H as she no feelings for me?

T ime for dinner, rummaging for her purse,
H as she finished, hope so, I'm bored?
E ventually she has finished.

E mptying my contents, looking for her phone,
Y esterday my head hurt through the constant drone,
E xactly as it stops ringing she answers with hello,
S o now she finished talking, back in it goes.

O nly as she gets out her make-up my headache goes away,
F inishing her make-up she puts it back in.

A nd now I'm starting to look a bit older!

H aven't seen the world before
A nd there's so much I want to see,
N o one understands what life is like for me!
D on't know what's going to be put in me next,
B ooks, make-up, phones and purses,
A nd much more you know,
G orgeous little bag unused, ripped torn and faded - stuck at the
Back of the cupboard all alone!

Laura Burnett (13)
Lord Lawson of Beamish School, Birtley

Through The Eyes Of Lebron James

Where am I? What am I doing?
There are people watching me
There are people staring at me.

As I step forward people clap
There is another team there
They are staring at me like
Wild boars.

When he goes in the tip I have a
Burst of energy as I sprint towards the basket,
I am overwhelmed
I am filled with excitement.

As the game draws to a near end
With only three to go
I run, I run
Like a nun going to pray
And then that is it,
It is all over.

We won, we won
All the excitement over
Like a bullet out of a gun.

Spent!

Christopher Curry (14)
Lord Lawson of Beamish School, Birtley

Through The Eyes Of A Schoolbag!

I'm dug out of the depths of a messy room,
Yet to face another day
Of being under table by table.

To my first table I go,
Not a clue where I'm going,
Where could it be?

As it gets darker and darker,
I feel the luke-warm atmosphere,
Seeping through my carefully textured finish.

To my next table I go,
Not a clue where I'm going
Where could it be?

Here it is cool and breezy,
Yet this floor under me is cold and hard,
How long left to go . . .?

To my next table I go,
Not a clue where I'm going,
Where could it be . . .?

Here there is no table,
Where could it be?

Nikki Davidson (13)
Lord Lawson of Beamish School, Birtley

Life As Obifemi Martins

I'm going to the training ground
Thinking about the last game
I don't flicker or make a sound.

Need to score a goal or the pressure piles up on me
I wish they could see what it's like
To be me I wish they could see.

I'm taking my penalty
Trying to steady myself mentally
That's it! I'm ready.

I think it's a great hit
But Cech catches it.

Jordan Dewhurst (14)
Lord Lawson of Beamish School, Birtley

Turn Back The Time

Turn back the clock, turn back the time.
Would it be different? Would it be bad?
Why did I do that crime!
I am so sorry, I am so sad!
The family so lonely, they always cry.
Pill by pill, woozier he got,
Why not me who had to die?
Two years later I feel like grot.

I told him to do it, I gave him advice.
People blame me for his death.
I thought I was helping a roll of the dice,
Weaker I get, breath by breath.

I will see him later at Heaven's gate.
His memories haunt me.
I will meet him again, but his heart's now filled with hate.
What can I do? What could it be?

If I forgot his life and thought of mine,
He would be healthy, honest and fine.

Turn back the clock, roll back the time.
So I don't ever do that crime!

Michael Dicks (13)
Lord Lawson of Beamish School, Birtley

Through The Eyes Of A Car

I'm driven to work then home,
Then to the garage alone,
I'm there all night in the freezing cold,

Even though I'm only one year old,
Then to work at twenty past,
I better drive there really fast.

And then straight home in the garage again
In the morning straight to the bank,
I better fill that twenty litre tank.

Now I'm over ten years old,
My wheels are rusty, I am cold,
My engine's broken, I'm being pushed.

I'm off to get my body crushed,
My life is over once and for all,
I won't be driven anymore.

Glenn Hayward (14)
Lord Lawson of Beamish School, Birtley

Life As A Subway Train

I always stay on track,
I travel forward and back.
I work all day,
I work all night,
If you cross me,
You may get a fright.

I carry you to work,
I carry you back,
I even pass that Hobo
Living in his shack.

If you run,
I'll close the doors,
Strange stains,
On the floor.

Adam Kavanagh (14)
Lord Lawson of Beamish School, Birtley

The Lonely Vampire

The vampire walking in the forest through the mud
All he could think about all day, was blood.
Then he remembered what it felt like at home,
Everybody fighting to use the phone.

In front of him he startled a cat
He got a shock and turned into a bat
A few yards further he flew and found a well
The darkness reminded him of the pits of Hell.

To not be a vampire is what he wished
To get out of this life that he got dished.
Suddenly the well began to glow
He turned into a boy and he felt his blood begin to flow.

His urge to kill and fight began to go away
No longer did he want to make his enemies pay.

Thomas Kitchen (14)
Lord Lawson of Beamish School, Birtley

Through The Eyes Of . . . A Happy Tree Friend

Up, higher than you can see,
There sits me the happy friend of trees,
With Pac Dan pupils and heart for noses,
As pink as fresh young roses.

I'm Giggles, all happy and glee,
You will never see a frown on me,
Unlike Flippy, who's good then bad,
One minute he's quiet, then he's pure mad.

I sit all day on flower-covered hills,
That was gone up by Jack and Jill,
I don't like to be lonely; it drives me round the bend,
Luckily I have so many friends.

Cuddles, Toothy and sneaky green Lifty,
Who I always get confused with his twin brother Shifty.
Petunia, Cub and scared little Flakey,
If I was you I wouldn't let him near any baking.

It's getting late, let's talk again soon,
I must get home before the sky meets the moon,
I have to go to sleep to rest my head,
It is always a fun day as a happy tree friend!

Samantha Lisle (14)
Lord Lawson of Beamish School, Birtley

Through The Eyes Of My Shoes

Through the eyes of my shoes
They are black with a bow
From heel to toe

At night they live in my closet
At day they live on my feet

They must see the world
From grass to my class
From birds and bees
To bugs and trees

I bought them just two weeks ago
As my other ones said no

They're shiny and new
But no they're not blue
They're small and petite
And no they're not cheap

They keep me dry in the rain
They keep me warm in the cold
In summer they keep me cool.

Stacie Maughan (14)
Lord Lawson of Beamish School, Birtley

Through The Eyes Of . . .

Through the eyes of my hat,
On top of my drawer it is sat,
I wear it out in winter when light is dim,
NY above the brim,
With a bright white trim,
I once lent it to Tim,
It's a good thing it can't hear,
But it's in one and out the other ear,
It's a dark blue colour,
But over time is getting duller,
It is getting old and about to fall apart,
But is still quite smart,
It's suited well when worn with a chain,
With a Staffy Pendant holding a cane,
Sometimes when I wear my hat people get the wrong impression,
Whenever I get pulled over they expect to hear a confession,
My hat suits anything - T-shirts and vests,
But with a hoody it looks best,
I have had my hat for quite a long time,
To me it's worth more than a dime.

Matty Nunn (13)
Lord Lawson of Beamish School, Birtley

My Poem

I hate it when I feel a person grabbing me,
A beautiful horse, that's all they can see.

As I try to run away,
All I want to do is play.

As I feel someone on top of me,
All I can feel is sweat dripping off me.

As I feel a hard whip,
I buck and bronk and then I trip.

Then I'm to run around like a slave;
As I am quite small, I feel brave.

I finally feel like I'm cooling down,
It's about time . . . I look like a clown.

As I get my drink and hay,
All I want to do is lay.

It never can be just right,
It's always hot, cold or shining bright.

My hooves are now very sore,
But now it's all a bore.

Then the day starts again,
As I got through the pain yet again!

Katie Pickup (14)
Lord Lawson of Beamish School, Birtley

Through The Eyes Of A Lazy Cat

All day long I sleep and sleep,
Mostly on the chair,
Or on the dirty washing heap.

Through the day I dream
Of tasty fish on a plate,
Or a fresh bowl of cream.

When the dark, dark night begins
And everyone's asleep
Alley cats of all ages meet around the bins.

They discuss what's happened on the news
Or what's been in the paper
Sometimes they talk about their favourite kitty kat chews.

Then the cats slink up to the wall
And start singing a tune
All cats all over Britain do this call.

Did I just see a squeaking mouse?
This will make my night
1 2 3 . . . pounce!

Soon it will be a very hot day
With the sun bright
And the moon tucked away.

So I will slink into my bed
And sleep through the hot day
For now the night is dead.

Katherine Saunders (13)
Lord Lawson of Beamish School, Birtley

The Good Old Days

I wish I could turn back time
To when I played out under the summer sky
Even though it felt like day
It was really night.

I wish I could turn back time
To when we never knew what enemies were
We all were friends
No falling out, the good old days.

I wish I could turn back time
To when we played in the paddling pool
We were all so happy
Splashing about in the hot summer sun.

I wish we could turn back time
So long ago
Plaiting hair at story time
When the teacher turned and looked away, the good old days.

I wish we could turn back time
Those good old days
Always smiley
Never a frown in sight
The good old days.

Hannah Smith (13)
Lord Lawson of Beamish School, Birtley

Through The Eyes Of . . .

Michael Dicks is my name
In the class I'm drinking Coke
Playing cricket is my game
Hitting sixes for a joke.

Every day after school
We're acting like fools
It's down to the fields
Using our bags as shields
Because I am the best
And I try to take down the rest
He tries to tackle us
Before we get the bus.

When I get home I go to training
But whenever I go it is raining
Wind or rain, sun or shine
Cricket is my favourite time.

Conor Young (14)
Lord Lawson of Beamish School, Birtley

Soldiers Of The Morning

Soldiers of the morning
Morning came and it started again,
The sound of gunshots and death all around,
Everywhere!
Soldiers bleeding . . . soldiers crying . . .
Soldiers weeping . . . and soldiers dying
The blistering heat of the sun belted the warriors
Scorching the battlefield
And bodies of the dead
Then so suddenly everything changed
The sun shied away and out
Came the rain.

Nathan Bastow (15)
Lord Lawson of Beamish School, Birtley

Challenging the Stereotypes Of Youth

Another day,
With nothing to do
Walking around,
With a friend or two.
Away from worries and problems
Having a laugh and
Going on daft,
To escape the reality of life.
It's good at the time,
And you appreciate your mates,
Learning from your own mistakes.
But another problem comes along;
Judgement.
Dirty looks from other people,
Fearful eyes from the old woman,
Who trembles past our group,
Automatically police assume we're trouble
Telling us to watch our backs.
Back to the park on a Friday night,
Away from everyone else.
Back with the people who don't have a go,
Because of who you are and what you know.

Laura Frank (15)
Lord Lawson of Beamish School, Birtley

Away Day

(We are the Geordie, the Geordie boot boys
We are mental and we are mad
We are the loyalest footballer supporters, the world has ever had)

That is the sound of the roar of the Geordies at match day,
They come in their masses to cheer their team on,
But if they lose there will be utter dismay.

Today is not any normal day,
Today is away day.

They travel in thousands from the north-east
Hoping that they will be able to defeat the beast.

One by one they enter the ground
But if anyone gets in their way they will give them a pound.

They cheer on their team hoping to win.

We are the Geordie, the Geordie boot boys.

Daniel Gaffney (14)
Lord Lawson of Beamish School, Birtley

Memories

Can you remember
That day at the park
The green grass, the tall tree
The soft sand, the cool sea?

Can you remember
That day at the zoo
The foul smell, the amount of food
The beaming sun, the cooling wind?

Can you remember
That day in the town
The smell of smoke, the boiling shops
The sound of tills, shopping till you drop?

Can you remember
I don't think you can . . .
But I can and always will.

Emma McCullen (15)
Lord Lawson of Beamish School, Birtley

Sick Bay

I sat in the sick bay all day,
Counting the minutes until the bell,
Cold and harsh in its toll,
Knelled the classes to an end.

Sitting here but for the hatred of a man
One who forced the monotony of the relay.
This hatred always in mind
Giving me strength to endure the boredom.

The metallic ring lifting my hopes,
Have them rise to the heavens,
The sport is over!
Only now to endure the rigidness of numbers.

Andrew Skeoch (15)
Lord Lawson of Beamish School, Birtley

Match Day

The roar of the masses,
Terrifying to all
The chants of the fans,
Inspiration to all.

The crowds lurch forward as one,
Desperate to enter the grounds
Utter chaos descends
An unstoppable ocean,
Of black and white.

I try to fight this unstoppable tide
But get pulled along with the invincible army
You cannot fight the flow.

We gather in droves at the turnstyles,
Chanting in ecstasy.
Eager for the match ahead
Minutes before kick-off
The stadium ripples like an angry ocean.

The players stream onto the pitch,
The whistle is blown
The ball is away
It is match day, hooray.

Andrew Swaddle (15)
Lord Lawson of Beamish School, Birtley

Flying

Flying, soaring, gliding through the crisp air,
High then low as wind blows away all cares.
Laughter and joyful screams echo from down below
The power to fly, yet nowhere to go.

The rusty frame squeaks and moves with every push,
But nothing, nothing can overcome the sound of soaring rush.
Trees, mountains and houses quickly come into sight,
Then quickly disappear, as though covered by the blanket of night.

Slowly, but surely the world around comes into clear view,
A soft breeze replacing the crisp wind that blew.
And all around no one ever understands what joy it can bring
The joy from a simple ride on a swing.

Maddy Thompson (15)
Lord Lawson of Beamish School, Birtley

Expectations

Why are we always made to look weak
When times in our lives are bleak?
Experience makes people stronger
But they have lived for longer.
Putting things into perspective
When they get too intensive;
Expectations are far too high
And all we can do is sigh . . .
Take a step back and think:
But never let yourself sink.
Just look to the future
And try to be mature -
Your problems will all be resolved.

Lauren Walton (15)
Lord Lawson of Beamish School, Birtley

I Am . . .

I am a ginger
My name is Scott
People would say that's it
I say not.

Our hair defines us
How it shimmers in light
People may insult us
I say they're not polite.

People say us gingers
We are all the same
People say we're angry
I can't complain.

But when people judge you
By the colour of your hair
It can make the strongest of us -
Even me - despair.

I may be ginger
But that's not the lot
I am proud of myself
And my name's Scott.

Scott Charlton (15)
Lord Lawson of Beamish School, Birtley

Crows

Those perfect girls sit like a circle of crows, cawing and cackling,
Their beady eyes, desperately searching for their next victim.
They ruffle their feathers, comparing
A hair out of place, a toe out of line
It is noticed.

The show goes on
Competition from others is eliminated
Stamped on, killed
They cannot bear to be upstaged.

It is a need, an obsession
They cannot stop.
Their beautiful soft feathers, their long talons
Picking, picking, picking at the vulnerable.

Sophie Wild (15)
Lord Lawson of Beamish School, Birtley

The World That We Live In

In the world we live in
Nobody's the same
Some people are poor
Some people have fame.

Somewhere in Africa
A parent is crying
Leaning over the bed
Of her child who is dying.

However somewhere else
A man's plotting away
Planning a murder that will take place
That very same day.

Millions of miles from there
A young teen's alone
She ran away
From the abuse of her home.

In a country not far off
A new baby is being born
Yet somewhere else in the world
Families are being torn.

So you see that our world is very different
From every place to place
You can see the joy or sorrow
In nearly everybody's face.

Hannah Bright (13)
Lord Lawson of Beamish School, Birtley

Treasure Box

I am like a treasure box
Though my feelings I must hide
Of these you cannot seek
They're buried deep inside.

I am like a treasure box
Your search is never-ending
I shall vow not to open
Unless on you I am depending.

I am like a treasure box,
Though my contents you shan't see
This I prefer kept private,
It is personal to me.

I am like a treasure box,
Though my feelings I must hide,
Of these you cannot seek,
They're forever locked inside.

Sammy Brown (13)
Lord Lawson of Beamish School, Birtley

Babies

Babies are so special
In their own way.
They always scream and cry,
But that happens every day.

Even though they tire you,
You can admit they do
They are so very cute,
But unfortunately you can't press mute.

Never underestimate them,
They're smarter than you think.
Make sure you never look away,
They could disappear in a blink.

They're always in your heart,
No matter how hard it is,
And if you bring them up well
You'll never drift apart.

Leah Cosgrove (12)
Lord Lawson of Beamish School, Birtley

Through The Eyes Of . . .

Mood swings like a roller coaster,
Can't control my thoughts
I'm up in the clouds
Then suddenly down below.

I didn't know what was wrong with me,
They sent me away for it.
They don't want me in their schools,
Just for being me.

They say I'm special
I hate to be this way.
I want to be normal
But I don't want their drugs.

Is it better to be alive,
When I'm like this?
If I can't be normal
Then should I be dead?

Eleri Cowlyn (12)
Lord Lawson of Beamish School, Birtley

Cars

F ast
E xciting
R ed
R acy
A ggressive
R ear-wheel drive
I nsane

B ugatti Veyron
U nrivalled performance
G ood on a track
A wesome power
T urbocharged 8.0 litre W16 engine
T en radiators to cool the engine
I nsane.

Christopher Douglas (13)
Lord Lawson of Beamish School, Birtley

The Bullies

T errorising young children
H arassing other students
E gging people's houses for fun.

B eating up people who are smaller than them
U sing kids by making them do things
L obbing stones at car windows
L aunching stones at young kids
I ntimidating people that they don't like
E vacuating the place where they committed a crime
S tealing from other people.

Thomas Dunn (13)
Lord Lawson of Beamish School, Birtley

My Poetry Lesson

I have no idea what to write
Even though, try as I might
The words just don't seem to want to come
It's like when I'm asked a really hard sum.

I can't think of what to write about
If someone can, please give me a shout
It's not that I'm stupid, dumb or thick
It's just that these things don't come quick.

I really hope I get paid for this
Oh no, oh dear, here comes Miss
I better put something down quick and fast
And after all that she walks straight past.
    Well that's not fair now, is it?

Claire Goodenough (13)
Lord Lawson of Beamish School, Birtley

Racism

R esponsible to stop it
A gainst human rights
C os some find it funny, but really it's sad
I nconsiderate for people's feelings
S imple-minded discrimination
M ocking and undermining.

Christian Harbison (13)
Lord Lawson of Beamish School, Birtley

This World

In this world there's loneliness
In this world there's happiness
Instead of hating everything.

Tear me from my skin
Tear me from my bones
Take me from this world and are you feeling
Happy now?

In this world there is love
But always surrounded by this darkness
With hate and sadness overwhelming.

Never lie, never die,
Gotta let this darkness in
Giving the world back from which I came from.

Brandon Howarth (13)
Lord Lawson of Beamish School, Birtley

Through The Eyes Of . . .

As I thunder over the hill,
Without saddle or bridle,
Only my free will,
Grass flows out
From under my hooves,
I have nothing I can lose.

The beat and rhythm
Round and round,
Is the only nearby sound.

I'm faster than the river,
Faster than flames,
Faster than the wind,
Which rushes through my mane.

No one has ever
Nailed horseshoes to my hooves
Or put a saddle on my back
So this certainly proves,

That I'm a wild horse
Fast and free
And you could never
Capture me.

Laura Kennedy (12)
Lord Lawson of Beamish School, Birtley

Dance

Every time I see dance,
It makes me want to join in,
But I know I must practice,
Put the commitment in.

But in my heart,
I know what I must do,
Strive for excellence,
It can't be that hard to do?

I mustn't lose my passion,
Keep the fire in my heart,
But when I hit the stage,
My passion falls apart.

I'm going to show what I can do,
I've come so far already,
I'm going to win the big cup too,
So everyone get ready.

Lauren Kirikal (12)
Lord Lawson of Beamish School, Birtley

Baby

Being a baby just isn't fair,
I've been left alone to stare and stare.
People brush past, they leave me alone,
It isn't fair, that I've got no home.

I go through the day,
Not knowing what's next,
I lie in the darkness,
Is my life hexed?

My cry is weak
So I try not to speak
I'm so badly bruised
For a good life I seek.

Lauren Malloy (13)
Lord Lawson of Beamish School, Birtley

A Tale Of Homeless Heartache

How am I supposed to live?
Just sitting on the floor
I've been doing this for one year now
Life's not the same anymore.

Every day has been the same
People either ignore me or say
'I wish she would just move'
Or 'She's always in the way.'

I can't help it that my life has changed,
That I'm now a homeless girl
I feel so awful every day
My life is in a whirl.

I ran away from home you see,
Away from that terrible place
Where I used to get a kick or a punch
Or worse, a slap in the face.

They've never tried to find me
I knew they didn't care.
I now hate the way people look at me
Some glance, some stop and stare.

Now every night I lie and dream,
About a nice new home
A family to love and cherish me,
And never leave me alone.

So now I hope you'll understand
That the homeless aren't a pain
We just want to be happy and well
And relive our lives again.

Laura Stipetic (12)
Lord Lawson of Beamish School, Birtley

The Race

Standing . . .
Nerves building up and up . . .
Jogging on the spot,
Stretching, warming up . . .
Waiting . . .
This is the big one . . .
Dreaming, floating . . .
Nerves building
Towering over the top.
Then the starter echoing the words
'On your marks'
Crouching on the start
Waiting . . . silence . . .
Then . . .
'Set'
Seeing the finish . . . only 100m away . . .
Then . . .
The gun . . . echoes as if from far away . . .
All of a sudden you're off . . .
Feet pounding the ground
You're shooting . . .
Flying . . .
Speeding towards the finish. Not long now
People sprinting behind you
The nerves left behind as you go faster . . . faster . . .
Feeling nothing . . . you want it . . .
Then it's over, you're 1st
People crossing the line after you
A golden, shiny medal thrust in your face
Glory.

Sophie Taylor (12)
Lord Lawson of Beamish School, Birtley

The Tree

I stand alone and solitary,
Sun beats down and warms me,
I shed my skin and watch it fall,
Graceful, silent and beautiful,
Bitter cold freezes me stiff,
Frost grasps me with brittle hands,
I can't escape,
Can't run away,
I just get on with life like I always have.

I stand tall and brilliant,
So much happens around me,
Joy, devastation and discovery,
The children climb,
So high, so far,
Into my tangled, twisted arms,
Then they fall, crying tears,
The laughter fades,
And time makes it a distant memory.

Helena Wallace (13)
Lord Lawson of Beamish School, Birtley

The World

In the world there are lots of people
Lots of churches with big tall steeples
Miles and miles of bare terrain
All eyes on Prime Minister's lane
Policemen and women patrolling the streets
Waiting to catch any thoughtless thieves
London's busy economy thriving
While people in Africa are dying
AIDS in Africa is a really big deal
If you had AIDS how would you feel?

Lewis Whybrow (13)
Lord Lawson of Beamish School, Birtley

The Kitchen Mess

Today I'm bored
Today there's nothing to do
Mum told me to go play out
But today it's raining too.

She won't be back for at least an hour
And there's rubbish on TV
There's not even any food to devour
And it's too early to make tea.

I'll try to make a milkshake
At least that'll be fun,
I'll turn on the oven
And heat some hot cross buns.

The lid on the blender's missing,
But I'm sure that won't matter.
The buns won't fit in the oven,
So I'll just make them flatter.

The milkshake's flying everywhere!
The oven's producing smoke!
The blender's knocked over the kitchen wear!
And I've just spilled my Coke.

I tried to fill a bucket,
But left the water running too long.
I tripped over the bin,
Cheese and mince makes such a pong!

The table's such a mess!
The floor's covered with crumbs!
Someone's opening the door
Oh no! It's Mum!

Carmel Woolmington (13)
Lord Lawson of Beamish School, Birtley

Legend

It was some time in May '05
When my thoughts and dreams came alive
My mam said, 'Son
We've won, we've won
And that this event would be fun.

As I listened
My eyes glistened
For I would be on TV
Standing next to David Batty,
I was mascot for the match.

We arrived at St James' Park
Not in light nor in dark
As the legends arrived
The crowd came alive
While I waited in the tunnel.

As we came out
The crowd gave a shout
Then the game begins.

The legends wins
The crowd sings
'Come on legends! Come on legends!'

Anthony Redhead (11)
Lord Lawson of Beamish School, Birtley

Homeless

I open my eyes,
It must be midday.
People are staring,
As there I lay.
They stare right through me,
They don't care, they don't know,
What is going through my mind,
Or how I got this low.
I sit day after day,
I'm given disgusted, hateful stares,
And all I'm thinking
As normal people stare,
What is the point?
People won't give,
All they give is pennies,
Assuming that's enough to live,
So why do I bother?
What is the benefit
Of binbag blankets,
Thrown away chicken bits,
Newspaper pillows?
Malnutrition round the corner
And dehydration,
Seeming closer and closer.
Watching people live,
From the pros to the novice,
Why don't I just end it?
No one would notice.

Vicki Hook (13)
Lord Lawson of Beamish School, Birtley

Brightly

Brightly the moon shines
Brightly the sun climbs
Brightly shines the cats' eyes
Brightly the metal shines in the sky
Brightly shine the street lights
Brightly shine the cars at night
Brightly the flowers grow in the park
Brightly my diamonds shine in the dark.

Emma Jones (12)
Teesside High School, Stockton-on-Tees

Loudly

Loudly the crowds scream.
Loudly the Hoover cleans.
Loudly the children play.
Loudly the Hindus pray.

Loudly the avalanche falls.
Loudly the bird calls.
Loud is the train - but loudest of all
Is the sound when the baby squalls.

Olivia Tindle (12)
Teesside High School, Stockton-on-Tees

Brightly

Brightly the diamond shines in light
Brightly the star shines in the night.
Brightly the cats' eyes shine at midnight
Brightly the car lights shine in the moonlight
Brightly the moon sits in the sky
Brightly the street lights light up the people going by.
Brightly the pearl shines in the middle of the ring
But brightest of all
Is the big orange ball.

Lucy Home (11)
Teesside High School, Stockton-on-Tees

Brightly

Brightly shines the moon in the sky,
Brightly shines the headlights passing by,
Brightly the cats' eyes glow in the dark,
Brightly the street lights flicker in the park,
Brightly the house windows shine with a glow,
Bright is the world as we all know.

Bright is the torch that shines in the night,
Bright is the eyes that jump with a fright,
Bright is the rain that splatters the road,
Bright is the lorry's heavy load,
Bright is the warm welcoming light,
From the house smothered in the deep black night.

Holly McCormack (11)
Teesside High School, Stockton-on-Tees

Cupid's Two Arrows

'Love like mine could never fade,
Just bloom in all of beauty's ways.'
'Love like mine has never been,
Love like yours, what do you mean?'
'Discouragement knows not my love,
It shines forever like stars above.'
'What I'll say I've said before,
Quite simply, leave, must I say more?'
'I could not move say what you will,
My love lives on, you cannot kill.'
'I do not care for what you say,
You are annoying, go away!'
'My love is armour, no harm you do,
I'll stay forever and wait for you . . .'

II

'My darling dear, are you in there?
I long to see your beauty fair.'
'Are you still here? So long you wait!
Can you please go, it's getting late.'
'I'll never leave I love you so,
To leave I'd die of endless woe.'
'I warn do not stay past your time,
I think I will call 999.'
'Call if you will, I do not care,
It's worth this time with you my fair.'
'Oh stop that now, I'll not be won
Go home at once and have some fun.'
'My self moves not, thy soul I breathe,'
'Shut up right now, I told you leave!'

Charlotte Howell (14)
Teesside High School, Stockton-on-Tees

Still Going

Name, Robert Rennison
Age, one hundred and two years
Number of memories, three hundred million.

I've seen a lot throughout my years,
The two World Wars, the telephone,
I've seen my wife grow up then die,
All my family too.

Yet here I am,
And here I am to stay
For at least another year.

What will I see?
More family go?
More family come?

How much I would love to go,
Once again out into the world,
To once again see the world in which I live,
To understand its changes,
To once again see the things I love.

But, here I am in my chair,
Here in this nursing home,
Struggling to hear,
The words my great granddaughter speaks.

Oh how I wish,
I wish so much
That I could be out there.

Alexandra Hamblett (14)
Teesside High School, Stockton-on-Tees

Life Is Only What You Make It

Beauty and destruction
Walk hand in hand.
Love and hate
Hold each other close,
Love and lust
Are long distant lovers.
Pain is best friends with relief.
A needle and thread can't fix a broken heart
As nothing can.
Luck is a wish never granted,
Life is only what you make it,
Perfect is a thing of the past,
When people didn't ask for so much.
Love means nothing without that warm feeling.
Help no longer exists
Life may be a lie
Love may be a sin
But power is nothing without sin
Smiles and tears can be fake,
And so can the people you *love.*

Sophie Stratford (13)
Teesside High School, Stockton-on-Tees

Brightly

Brightly shone the moon that night,
Brightly in the dazzling candlelight.
Brightly fireworks flash in the sky,
Brightly reflecting in the cat's sparkling eyes.

Brightly diamonds shine in the sun,
Brightly people play for fun.
Brightly in the fiery candlelight,
Shines the silver locket tonight.

Claire McKenna (12)
Teesside High School, Stockton-on-Tees

Quietly

Quietly the cat creeps by
Quietly the birds fly
Quietly people pray
Quietly ships wait at bay.

Quietly people sleep
Quietly I weep
Quiet is a mouse
But quietest of all
Is the silence of the fall.

Akriti Nanda (12)
Teesside High School, Stockton-on-Tees

The World Is . . .

The world is a ball of different colours,
Whizzing through time and space.
The world is an orb full of light and love,
None of which goes to waste.
The world is a magical sphere,
That captures the beauty of man and child.
The world is a globe that encloses,
Mysterious creatures with tempers ever so mild.

The world is a place,
Full of poverty and despair.
The world is a terrible beast,
That gives people great scares.
The world is a cruel monster,
That spits out deadly waves,
The world is a fiend,
That burps out earthquakes.

The world is full of jokes and laughter,
The world is for you and me hereafter.
The world is full of smiles and frowns,
So turn that frown upside down.

Khunsha Cheema (12)
Teesside High School, Stockton-on-Tees

Last Memories

The sound of the wind,
The bright morning sun,
Is all he can think of,
Except for the gun.

His little boy Jack,
And his two-year-old girl,
Is all he can think of,
Back home, safe, as she twirls.

His dad who passed away,
His wife who died peacefully
Is all he can think of,
As he gazes at the memories thoughtfully.

The last thought is for his mother
All alone except for his children,
Left to care for one another,
The time has come for him to go
And then the big gun suddenly goes boom!

Pooja Moonka (13)
Teesside High School, Stockton-on-Tees

My Valentine

A day with you is a day in Heaven
A moment that I do cherish so dear,
I shall not leave 'til the strike of seven
For by the eve I must depart, I fear
That should I too long in thy presence stay,
Thy special beauty may lose me my sleep,
Commend me thy heart, I long for this day,
I'll wait 'til the ends of time and believe,
As I am enchanted under your gaze,
And lost in your mysterious dark eyes,
While all the world is nothing but a haze,
That someday, my silent love is realised.
An answer doth lie in your heart, so fine
So I'll ask: Willst thou be my valentine?

Chetna Sharma (14)
Teesside High School, Stockton-on-Tees

Non-Rhyming Poem

He shoots, he scores
The game that's top notch
Football is like the heavens above
They dive as if they have been shot
It's not the players that make the beautiful game.

He slots the penalty home
That makes it 4-4 on penalties
The beautiful game spoilt by penalties
But nevertheless it still has to be won.

Hoorah, hoorah, hoorah
He scores the goal at Wembley to win the game
They are the champions
But the beautiful game never ends.

Ross Sawyers (14)
St Bede's Catholic Comprehensive School, Peterlee

Non-Rhyming Poem

The sun is hot,
And she's in the garden sunbathing.
Her brother is playing football,
While her mam is doing the barbecue,
And her sister is in the paddling pool.
She's getting a nice tan,
While she's in the garden.
She can smell the food and she starts to get hungry,
Her mam calls her for lunch.
She grabs a plate and fills it up.
Her brother does the same thing.
She lies back down on her towel, eating her food,
Until her brother throws water over her.
She gets up and screams at her brother,
She gets sent in and she sits by her window wishing to
Come back out.

Hannah-Leigh Westgarth (13)
St Bede's Catholic Comprehensive School, Peterlee

Rhyming Poem

The time in the year comes,
Where children go crying to their mums.
Wanting ice cream,
With a multicolour theme.
But parents are just sitting twiddling their thumbs.

Leaves as green as ever,
And teenagers thinking they are clever.
Throwing water bombs,
And running into Tom's.
Then being told that they are grounded forever.

Swimming pools come out,
So people begin to shout.
Water is running in
While children run about with wet skin.
They run the wrong way so take a different route.

Leanne Newton (14)
St Bede's Catholic Comprehensive School, Peterlee

Road To The Championship

The footy match was on,
And everyone was watching
The telly was loud
And everyone was shouting
People were enthusiastic
And wanted their team to win.

People were patient
As they waited for a goal
As the players ran up the pitch
Everyone stood up
He shoots,
He scores
And the crowd go wild!

As the whistle sounded at the end of the game
The team ran off winning the match
People were pleased and jumped up and down
As now they have gone to the Championship.

Lauren Parkin (14)
St Bede's Catholic Comprehensive School, Peterlee

Coffee

Alarm goes off; I crawl out of bed,
Put on the kettle to sort out my head.
Coffee or tea, what will it be?
Latte, mocha or espresso for me?

Decisions, decisions, it's all too much,
Too little sleep I've lost my touch.
Coffee it is and I reach for my mug,
The first little gulp is as warm as a hug.

I sit in my chair and curl up my feet,
Reaching for biscuits, I so love to eat.
At first I was lost in my morning daze,
But now thanks to coffee I've cleared the haze.

Johanna Wood (14)
St Bede's Catholic Comprehensive School, Peterlee

One Day

One day I'll be famous,
Or will I?
One day I'll be popular,
Or will I?
One day I'll be pretty,
Or will I?
One day I'll be an icon,
Or will I?
One day I'll achieve something big,
I know that for sure . . .

Nicola Graham (13)
St Bede's Catholic Comprehensive School, Peterlee

Bazza

B right you stand out
A ppreciated by all
Z zzz, rest in peace Bazza
Z zzz, rest in peace Bazza, goodnight
A lways loved forever.

Natalie Smith (13)
St Bede's Catholic Comprehensive School, Peterlee

Stars

S parkling so bright
T winkling in the sky
A ll around lots of gorgeous stars
R ays of light
S tars so bright.

Jade Naylor
St Bede's Catholic Comprehensive School, Peterlee

Haikus

Wolves stood on a cliff
Howling at the yellow moon
Music to my ears.

Wolves are beautiful
Lying on the ground at night
Under the bright moon.

Teeth as sharp as blades
Wandering through the forest
Searching for their prey.

Large, soft and furry
People think they're soft as muck
But they're vicious.

Lying on a cliff
With the moon shining on them
They look beautiful.

When they catch their prey
They shred it into pieces
Don't get close to them.

They have brill eyesight
To sneak on an animal
They've got good hearing.

People can't see them
Because they are camouflaged
Into the white snow.

They live in the snow
In the terrible weather
That is where they live.

Emma Dixon (13)
St Bede's Catholic Comprehensive School, Peterlee

Friends

F riends last a lifetime
R elying on one another
I f one's down
E verybody cheers them up
N ever alone or sad
D ays together are fun with laughter
S haring secrets and gossip.

Sarah Little (14)
St Bede's Catholic Comprehensive School, Peterlee

Loneliness

L ying on the ground
O nly thing I wish for is a best friend
N obody seems to care
E veryone is unaware
L ying alone on the ground
I nto the emptiness I yell
N obody's listening
E verybody's gone
S omeone love me
S omeone see me!

Stacey Hall (14)
St Bede's Catholic Comprehensive School, Peterlee

Gears Of War

G ears of war
E ven more fun
A great game
R apidly reloading
S cary

O utstanding
F un

W ell good
A drenaline rush
R ealistic.

Christopher Renwick (13)
St Bede's Catholic Comprehensive School, Peterlee

Hedgehogs - Haikus

Small, shy and spiky
Curl up in a little ball
To hide and be safe.

Gorgeous when first born
In danger when on the road
Hedgehogs are so cute.

Little button nose
And with tiny beady eyes
They search for their prey.

A hole in the tree
Lies the hedgehog sound asleep
In the autumn leaves.

Ashleigh Purcell (13)
St Bede's Catholic Comprehensive School, Peterlee

Poem

L ittle steps he takes when he runs
E very day he makes me laugh
W hy does he always act stupidly
I think he's a canny lad
S port, he is very good at.

David Hughes (13)
St Bede's Catholic Comprehensive School, Peterlee

I Love . . . Poem

L iving
O ut
V igorous
E motions.

Hannah Webster (14)
St Bede's Catholic Comprehensive School, Peterlee

Holidays

H aving fun
O n the beach
L aughing loudy
I n the sun
D ays go by
A s the holiday closes
Y esterdays over now
S o bring on tomorrow.

Sarah Golden (13)
St Bede's Catholic Comprehensive School, Peterlee

Untitled

'First it started with a kiss
How did it end up like this
It was only a kiss?'

I thought it would last forever
The love we share
Me and you together
But my heart you had to tear.

The days we spent
Never seemed to end
I shed a tear when you went
When you told me I was only a friend.

The heart that was once whole
Now turned cold
As I was once told
As the lies were unfolded.

'It started with a kiss
How did it end up like this
Ending with a tear . . .'

Danielle Lister (14)
St Bede's Catholic Comprehensive School, Peterlee

Love, Chocolate And More Love

Love is like a chocolate bar,
It melts your heart away,
This is what I came to say,
I love you on this sunny day.

Every time I see you,
A smile comes on your face,
It makes me so happy,
To know
That in your heart I have the only place.

It's quite hard to bear
The chocolate is now gone
Sadly it has to end
Until another weekend.

Emma-Jo Blundy (12)
Woodham Community Technology College, Newton Aycliffe

Love

I've got this peculiar feeling,
That I've never felt before,
I can't seem to get rid of it,
I guess it's here to stay,
I hope you feel in your heart,
That this is just the start,
I'm admitting to one thing,
I guess it's called a fling,
I'm putting myself on the line,
It's for you so it is fine.

Sarah Butler (11)
Woodham Community Technology College, Newton Aycliffe

Death By School

School
Or a never-ending torture
Eternal suffering
Dragged across a carpet
Lots of carpet burns
Lots of pain
Screaming
Shouting
Crying
. . .
. . .
. . .
Then you go home.

Karl Beaton (12)
Woodham Community Technology College, Newton Aycliffe

Love

I stand and watch
Just wait and stare
Always hoping you will be there
One day wishing my dream will come true
All it is is to be with you
As you walk past my heart skips a beat
Too shy to look in your eyes
My head drops to your feet
Love is a word that is shared by two
Love is wonderful, love is you!

Jessica Greenwood (12)
Woodham Community Technology College, Newton Aycliffe

Space

What mysteries lie beyond,
What we see in the night sky?
Are there UFOs and intelligent beings?
Do aliens above us fly?

Where does a black hole lead?
A giant, sucking mouth,
Full of greed.

How did it start?
Was it with a crash or a bang,
Or was it God - as all the angels sang?

I guess we will never know,
Are we alone?
Are we alone?

How big is the universe - way up there?
Where so many people just sit and stare,
At the night sky with awe and wonder,
Earth is also full of amazing things,
Waterfalls, wildlife, lightning, thunder,
All these things make us wonder.

Are we alone?
We will never know,
Are we alone,
Are we alone?

Callum David Scott (12)
Woodham Community Technology College, Newton Aycliffe

My Poem

I like dogs that run and play,
I like cats that sleep all day,
I like birds when they fly around,
I like snakes that slither along the ground.

I like horses because they are strong,
They pull ploughs all day long,
I like sheep, they give us wool,
They also keep our tummies full.

Dogs that I know are kind,
They never seem to mind,
How far we walk each day,
They think it's just play.

Pet rabbits are so soft and warm,
I could not let them come to harm.
I feed mine once a day,
And change their bed of hay.

Elephants should not live in zoos,
In ones and twos,
India or Africa they should home
Where they have miles of space to roam.

Slugs and snails are slimy and shiny,
Worms and caterpillars too,
I am kind to spiders and ladybirds
Because of the good things they do.

Simon Howe (11)
Woodham Community Technology College, Newton Aycliffe

Wailing Widow

Beware of the wailing widow!
She will freeze you with her unearthly howl.
Grinding you to a halt,
She will drift closer and closer,
Then you know that you're lost.
She sucks your soul out and into her,
Then she floats away,
What about your body?
Limp and lifeless it lies forgotten for evermore.

Jessica Mason (11)
Woodham Community Technology College, Newton Aycliffe

Ellie

'We've got a secret' said Mam and Dad
'We think you'll be surprised but really glad'
'We're getting a dog,' we shouted with glee
'Not even close, cos it's a baby!'

Oh my God, how fat is Mum!
Her belly's enormous and so is her bum!
Not long now until the big day arrives
And we can meet our special surprise!

The baby is now three days late
How much longer do we have to wait?
Mam's in hospital we've really missed her
Hip hip hooray, we've got a sister!

Aimee Green (12)
Woodham Community Technology College, Newton Aycliffe

One Winter's Night

A silent night so sweet and sound,
Snowflakes drifting to the ground.
The whole world sleeping, no one awake,
What patterns on the windowpane will the frost make?

The fire crackling releasing heat,
The young squirrel foraging for berries to eat.
Stars twinkling in the misty sky,
The red-breasted robin flies swiftly by.

The choir singing about the street,
Walking around on weary feet.
The bare trees shuddering in the cold,
A traditional celebration is going to unfold.

Everyone gathered around the fire,
Hearts filled with a loving desire.
Sins and bad feelings are strictly banned,
Because it's a Christmas wonderland.

Emily Small (11)
Woodham Community Technology College, Newton Aycliffe

Recycling Poem!

I use the kerb-it recycles bin almost every day,
To tidy old tins and bottles, which will be
Used another day.
I put all my old newspapers in,
Telephone directories too,
Magazines and comics
Leaflets and flyers will do.
It really, really helps the world,
Other countries too,
To recycle old rubbish this helps me and you.
So please put out your kerb-it bin, please
Please do, as it will help the universe
Through and through and through.

Hannah Pearson (12)
Woodham Community Technology College, Newton Aycliffe

Kos

From bubble beach . . .
Minerals arose;
But no lava shows;
Hotels amazing;
Locals crazing;
Creatures creeping;
Widows weeping;
The party mood;
Lovely food;
Shimmering sun burning;
Tourists learning;
Speedboats speeding;
Reps leading;
The hotel 5 star;
Driving a 4 x 4 car;
The army tying knots;
Then loud shots;
A flight delay;
Then flying over the bay . . .

. . . away.

Callum Gibb-Lenahan (11)
Woodham Community Technology College, Newton Aycliffe

In The Eyes Of A Fish

All I see all day is $H^2 0$ in my way,
Darting down the river with nothing but fishermen to spoil my day.
Alas, I am a freshwater trout
I do nothing all day but jump about
I need water - lots to survive, but those humans pollute it,
Cursing me to die,
So there is one last thing to say!
'Stop destroying my water and taking my freedom away!'

Andrew Turnbull (11)
Woodham Community Technology College, Newton Aycliffe

The Despair Of The Spectacled Bear

She smelt their scent on the forest air,
They're coming.
They're coming.
She heard their footfall through the trees,
Fear coming.
Fear coming.
She heard their voices calling more,
Pain coming.
Pain coming.
She saw the merciless stare in their eyes,
It had begun.
It had begun.
She felt her cub tremble against her chest,
Tears coming.
Tears coming.
She saw their hands reach out and take,
Loss coming.
Loss coming.
She lurched forward and attacked,
Anger burning.
Anger burning.
She felt the bullet in her side,
Death coming.
Death coming.
She heard her cub call for her help,
Pain coming.
Pain coming.
She saw her cub taken away, doomed by cruelty forever.
We need your help. We need your help.

Sian Hutchings (13)
Wolsingham Comprehensive School, Wolsingham

Growing Up

Growing up - the end of innocence.
When you're against the world
And the world's against you.

You're not accepted as yourself,
You've got to adopt a label,
To change, just to fit in.

To them you're just another person in the world
Unless you act like them
Dress like them
Look like them.

The world is meant to be different,
Not filled with the same people
Don't make yourself up.
Don't act like the rest.

But you're only what you make yourself
So how does the world change you so easily?

Tessa Mottram (13)
Wolsingham Comprehensive School, Wolsingham

Access Denied

You cannot preserve me
I am not yours to keep
No matter what you say
Or what you do.

I am not yours

I had a life of my own
Until you arrived
I had confidence of my own
Until you arrived
I knew how to trust
Until you arrived
You muttered the words 'You are mine'
When you arrived.

You . . .
So possessive. So violent. So hurtful
Me . . .
So scared. So stupid. So gullible.

I feel as big as you make me feel
Which most of the time is small
Smaller and smaller I shrink until . . . I am nothing.

Then I knew it was time for me to spread my wings
And see what's on the other side
I'd heard the grass was greener
But my access had always been denied.

My legs are sore and bleeding, no one was there to help
I doubt that I was being selfish when I went to help myself by . . .

Walking out the door and passed you to mutter
I am not yours . . . you looked at me but did not move
So I decided to take my chance and set you straight once and for all
So I continued . . . and you were never mine . . .

Emma Kelly (13)
Wolsingham Comprehensive School, Wolsingham

Nightingale

Nightingale,
Singing softly,
Beneath the cherry-blossom tree.
Filling people's hearts with joy,
Silently happy,
In the sun.
Not a care in the world.

Now I know,
That I can't sing
As well as a
Nightingale,
But still I sing,
And still I try,
Hoping that one day,
I'll fill someone else's
Heart with joy.

Nightingale,
Singing softly
Beneath the cherry-blossom tree
And gently then,
It spreads its wings
And flies away,
Filling someone else's
Heart with joy.

Tamsin Rees (13)
Wolsingham Comprehensive School, Wolsingham

Spot The Difference!

Here I am thinking,
While my dog is weeping,
How tall am I?
How small my dog is,
Why is my dog so colourful?
Why am I not more than one colour?
Why do I have a better life than my dog?
All my dog does is exercise and play
What an easy life for her,
What a hard life for me,
Can you spot the difference,
Between me and her?
Guess what? My dog is called Spot.

Jayne Dobson (13)
Wolsingham Comprehensive School, Wolsingham

Emotions

Blue as a sky means a tear from your face
As it drops to the floor it tastes salty
And bitter and then it turns raw.

Red as some blood means warm tender love,
It creeps up from nowhere and is as beautiful as a dove.

Black as a shadow means horrible fear,
Moves right behind you and sometimes causes a tear.

Yellow as the sun, means happiness all day long,
Prancing round in your garden, maybe singing a song.

White as a piece of paper means no emotions at all;
Even though fear is scary
This is the worst of all.

Libby Flannagan (12)
Wolsingham Comprehensive School, Wolsingham

We're All Different In The End

He has blond hair
But she has brown.

He lives in a city
But she lives in a town
We're all different in the end.

He has blue eyes
But she has green.

He is an adult
But she is a teen
We're all different in the end.

He is blind
But she still walks slowly behind.

He committed murder
But she never got the chance because he never heard her
We're all different in the end.

I just walked along that street
And personally I'm beat.

Now I've turned around the bend
None of that was pretend
We're all different in the end.

Anna Tidyman (12)
Wolsingham Comprehensive School, Wolsingham

The Sky . . .

Why do I look up to the sky?
There is still war and poverty in the world,
Why do I look up to the sky?
There is still pain and grief in the world,
Why do I look up to the sky?
There are still people dying and suffering today,
Why do I look up to the sky?
I know why, because when I look up to the sky
Already the world seems a friendlier place.
The sky helps me through
Why do I look up to the sky?
The sky is my family,
That is why.

Olivia Hodgson (12)
Wolsingham Comprehensive School, Wolsingham

School

I go to school what seems like every day, it's boring,
I go in and do the work again and again, it's boring,
I go to lunch and have the same every day, it's boring,
I go in the yard with my friends again and again, it's boring,
I go to school on the bus, the same every day, it's boring,
I go in the library and talk with my friends again and again, it's boring,
I go to school again and again, what seems like every day,
School is boring.

Thomas Oliver (12)
Wolsingham Comprehensive School, Wolsingham

I See, I See

I see, I see, what looks
To be sheep in the meadow.

I see, I see, what looks
To be a cow in the barn alone.

I see, I see, what looks
To be a pig rolling around
In the mud.

I see, I see, what looks
To be chickens pecking
Around in the straw for seed.

I see, I see what looks
To be ducks sat on the pond.

I see, I see what looks
To be the end of you
And me.

Thomas Williamson (13)
Wolsingham Comprehensive School, Wolsingham

Can't Speak Or Won't

'Hello'
. . .
'What is your name?'
. . .
'OK, so you don't want to talk to me,'
'Ummm'
'Just say something, I won't tell.'
'I . . .'
'What?'
'But I'm scared of what people might think.'
'What do you mean?'
. . .
'You're just the same as the rest of us.'
'No I'm not.'
'Well tell me I won't say anything.'
'I don't want to speak.'
'What?'
. . .

Rob Burleigh (13)
Wolsingham Comprehensive School, Wolsingham

I Only Want One Thing

Christmas is coming soon,
I love Christmas.
Each year I make a list
My list, is small.

I only want one thing,
But never will I get it.

I write the list in dark,
Not seeing it.
Writing same thing each year,
My list, is tiny.

I only want one thing,
But never will I get it.

I only want my sight,
Surely that's not too much.

Callum Hall (13)
Wolsingham Comprehensive School, Wolsingham

That Memory

Every day
I wake up with that same memory
It was the day the Germans came
We hid some Jews
But some could not hide
They were kicked and shoved
Treated like animals
My friend was a Jew
I never saw him again
That night I helped them escape
But those horrible people found them
I just got away.

Callum Hodgson (12)
Wolsingham Comprehensive School, Wolsingham

High Hopes

To stand tall you need high hopes,
But my hopes stand me small,
What does it take to have hopes that stand on ladders?

A moment of dull sickness,
As my foot misses a step.
But my hand clings desperately on.

Nails are chipped, confidence smashed,
Eyes see only the top.
But this ladder has a long way down.

Heart pounds inside my chest
Mind drifting . . .
My other hand clings desperately on,
And this time I move up.

Nails are grown,
Confidence regained.
Mind sailing on a white-tipped sea,
And my heart goes easy on my chest.

To stand tall you need high hopes,
And my hopes stand up high
A metaphor used to describe you touching the sky.

Georgia Maddison (13)
Wolsingham Comprehensive School, Wolsingham

The Packet Of Tablets

You're at a party, dancing alone,
Along came a man, some paper he'd shown.
'Inside are some tablets, they're good for your health,'
You give him the money, building his wealth.
You take one of the tablets and you feel fine,
Then your head starts spinning with a groaning whine.
You're walking home with a packet by your side,
You don't see the lamp post and then you collide.
You're lying on the floor, vomiting, screaming,
The tablets are bad, your forehead is steaming.
You find yourself addicted to these,
You shove one in your mouth, willing to please.
You lie awake, cannot seem to sleep,
With those tablets you cannot keep.
You're walking to the balcony, looking below,
Your head feels so bad, you're about to blow.
You stand on the bars, willing to jump,
You fall off the edge and land in a clump.
A man comes along, sees that you're dead,
And a packet of tablets right next to your head.
Ecstasy is the worst drug in the world,
Where you lie on the floor, toss and twirl.
Your body is filling with many nasty bugs,
You've learnt your lesson, don't do drugs.

Diane Beddard (12)
Wolsingham Comprehensive School, Wolsingham

Disappearing Act

What is it like to be lifeless?
With no power.
To reach out. To feel nothing.
Plagued by your demons.
All that time to reflect.

You just want to forget.
To be left alone.
You're leached of your colour.
Bleeding from your self-inflicted wound.
Wanting to disappear.
The world's pain and anger in your head.

You couldn't stop. Why?
That's the way it works.
Your family in tears,
And yet you feel nothing.
You stare blankly,
Wishing for it all to go away.

It's all your fault,
You could have got help.
But you chose not to.
And now it's too late.

Almost.

Roisin Taylor (12)
Wolsingham Comprehensive School, Wolsingham

Empty

I sit in the dark,
Cold and alone,
Empty inside,
Chilled to the bone.

I hear the grass whisper,
As the wind speaks my sorrowed story,
The trees glare, the flowers stare.

The rain cages me in an isolated cell,
Nowhere to run, nowhere to hide,
Why bother trying,
When all I have in me is pain,
Pain always, pain forever.

The hands of the moon reach out,
Like wisps of silver smoke,
To throttle, to kill.

I welcome them, welcome death,
But no,
They know my wish,
Instead they do their worst,
They doom my body forever.

Surge their hands into my chest,
And capture my distressing heart,
Then yank it out of me,
Take my light away,
Leave me to live,
To live forever as an emotionless monster,
Nothing but a vessel.

I sit in the dark,
Cold and alone,
Empty inside chilled to the bone . . .

Naomi Sheville (13)
Wolsingham Comprehensive School, Wolsingham

Hurt

Hide
I hide when they are angry or sad
Though I hide when they are happy too.

Because I make them angry

They like weapons
They like bats and balls and socks
But it doesn't matter what they use

It all makes me suffer

They leave me in the rain
They don't care, I don't feel
Because I am just an object they can

Kick, hit, blame

People tried to take
Take me away to somewhere safe
But I was not allowed

They know that for sure

They claimed me
They chained me so I could not move
And then they took a knife
And stick and mallet and stone

And then I did not move.

Misha Monkman (13)
Wolsingham Comprehensive School, Wolsingham

Young Writers Information

We hope you have enjoyed reading this book - and that you will continue to enjoy it in the coming years.

If you like reading and writing poetry drop us a line, or give us a call, and we'll send you a free information pack.

Alternatively if you would like to order further copies of this book or any of our other titles, then please give us a call or log onto our website at www.youngwriters.co.uk

Young Writers Information
Remus House
Coltsfoot Drive
Peterborough
PE2 9JX

(01733) 890066